D1929921

How to Get Published in Anthropology

A Guide for Students and Young Professionals

Edited by
Jason E. Miller
and
Oona Schmid

ALTAMIRA
PRESS

A division of
ROWMAN & LITTLEFIELD PUBLISHERS, INC.
Lanham • New York • Toronto • Plymouth, UK

Published by AltaMira Press
A division of Rowman & Littlefield Publishers, Inc.
A wholly owned subsidiary of The Rowman & Littlefield Publishing Group, Inc.
4501 Forbes Boulevard, Suite 200, Lanham, Maryland 20706
http://www.altamirapress.com

Estover Road, Plymouth PL6 7PY, United Kingdom

Copyright © 2012 by AltaMira Press

All rights reserved. No part of this book may be reproduced in any form or by any electronic or mechanical means, including information storage and retrieval systems, without written permission from the publisher, except by a reviewer who may quote passages in a review.

British Library Cataloguing in Publication Information Available

Library of Congress Cataloging-in-Publication Data
How to get published in anthropology : a guide for students and young professionals / edited by Jason E. Miller and Oona Schmid.
p. cm.
Includes bibliographical references.
ISBN 978-0-7591-2108-9 (pbk. : alk. paper) —
ISBN 978-0-7591-2109-6 (electronic)
1. Anthropology—Authorship—Marketing. 2. Social science literature—Publishing. 3. Mass media and anthropology—Marketing. I. Miller, Jason E., 1981– II. Schmid, Oona, 1970–
GN307.7.H69 2011
301—dc23 2011036185

∞™ The paper used in this publication meets the minimum requirements of American National Standard for Information Sciences—Permanence of Paper for Printed Library Materials, ANSI/NISO Z39.48-1992.

Printed in the United States of America

Contents

Preface v

Introduction: What Is Publishing? vii
Oona Schmid

PART I: STEP-BY-STEP GUIDANCE AND ADVICE

1 Attending Conferences and Organizing a Panel 2
Jason E. Miller

2 Creating and Presenting an Academic Poster 12
John K. Trainor

3 Presenting a Paper 24
Paul N. Edwards

4 Submitting and Getting an Article Accepted in a Journal 38
Tom Boellstorff

5 Publishing Your Dissertation as a Monograph 49
Sarah Caro

PART II: SUBDISCIPLINARY CONSIDERATIONS

6 Archaeology 60
William Green and Linda Forman

7 Applied and Public Anthropology 70
Tim Wallace

8 Biological and Physical Anthropology 79
Paul A. Garber

9 Cultural/Social Anthropology and Ethnography 88
Catherine Besteman

10 Linguistic Anthropology 95
Mary Bucholtz

11 Medical Anthropology 103
Linda M. Whiteford and Cecilia Vindrola Padros

12 Visual Anthropology 112
Peter Biella

PART III: GENERAL DISCUSSIONS

13 Author Agreements 126
Ricky S. Huard

14 Copyright 134
Peter Givler

15 Collaboration 143
Don Brenneis

16 Online Opportunities and Challenges 151
Hugh W. Jarvis

Appendix A: Peer-Reviewed Journals 163

Appendix B: Publishers That Publish Anthropology Monographs 167

About the Editors and Contributors 169

Preface

Within days of assuming our posts as director of publishing and as president of the student chapter at the American Anthropological Association, it quickly became obvious that relatively few graduate students receive consistent, current, and correct intelligence about publishing. These impressions are corroborated by researchers at the University of Washington School of Education. Their 2008 survey quantifies this need: whereas 432 anthropologist Ph.D.s lauded their graduate programs for teaching them critical-thinking skills and data analysis, the majority commented that they had received "poor" or "adequate" preparation in skills like writing, publishing, and presenting. Thus, we hope graduate students, their advisors, and newly minted anthropologists will all find this resource useful. It should reduce stress and uncertainty and increase practical knowledge about how to publish, why to publish, and which publishing efforts will mean the most in the long run.

This book addresses these needs in three ways. In part I, chapters provide step-by-step instruction and details about how to accomplish specific aims. We focused on the efforts that the widest number of young anthropologists may benefit from, namely organizing a panel, presenting at a scholarly conference, submitting to a journal, and turning a dissertation into a monograph. No chapter in the book requires reading other chapters, so each of these tutorials may be consulted at the time when young scholars begin to think, "How exactly do I go about accomplishing this activity?"

In part II, chapters provide personal narratives about observations from within the main subdisciplines. These texts are firsthand accounts and take a more emic approach. The chapters will hopefully elucidate some of the subfields' nuances and assist young anthropologists in maximizing their attentions in the ways that subfield peers may particularly value. These chapters differ by the personality of the authors but generally counsel how to maximize the chances of getting hired and promoted by an academic committee from the standpoint of anthropologists who have "made it."

Finally, part III addresses more advanced concerns that may vex more experienced writers including commentaries on collaborating with others when writing, copyright issues, and online opportunities and threats.

Much more could be said about any one of these topics. As editors, we tried to make sure terms are clear to even the least experienced students. We sought to keep chapters succinct and encouraged authors to include a "Further Reading" section at the end of each chapter.

Finally, we encouraged a lighthearted approach, and many of the authors obliged us. Publishing is serious business, but like many matters in life, we hope it is also a joy.

Jason E. Miller
Oona Schmid

Introduction

What Is Publishing?

Oona Schmid

Most of this book focuses on *how* young scholars should go about getting published in anthropology, but some readers want still more basic questions answered: Why should I publish? or What constitutes publishing? This introduction offers some broad reasons to publish, defines scholarly publishing in its rapidly changing contexts, and summarizes some criteria for what constitutes "prior publication."

WHY PUBLISH?

Most academic hiring and promotion committees want three things in their candidates: publications, service, and teaching. Different schools weigh these endeavors differently, with some institutions placing tremendous value on front-of-classroom performance by asking candidates to give a guest lecture to the interviewing body and submit a sample syllabus, and by examining student evaluations. However, virtually all tenure-track positions consider the candidate's publishing record. This usually includes scrutinizing the resume for prestigious and peer-reviewed publications. At large research-focused universities (the institutions that grant Ph.D.s in anthropology, for instance), publishing is the sine qua non—the essential ingredient—and may be the primary consideration in hiring and tenure. Increasingly at all colleges, the weight and focus on publications has increased. In 2008, the American Anthropological Association asked 226 department chairs about tenure. One respondent wrote, "The importance of scholarship to tenure has grown unofficially. The College has hired enormous numbers of new tenure-track faculty since 2000, who generally are more research oriented. Expectations of scholarly production have risen without any formal change to tenure policy."

For anthropologists looking for jobs outside of the academy, publishing does not have as privileged a role, but a publishing track record confirms your expertise in your area and makes your application particularly interesting to the hiring manager or committee.

So what does publishing entail that signals such value to hiring gatekeepers? The answer is threefold: publication validates your work, furnishes you with credit for your ideas, and fulfills an obligation to share your ideas and enrich scholarly discourse.

First, publishing in peer-reviewed publications means that other readers with knowledge in your area (your peers) have validated your work and given it a stamp of approval as new, significant, and valuable to the scholarly record. In other words, the activities that surround publishing such as peer review and the processes of selecting and polishing content all help to ensure the spread of *good* ideas. The chapters in part II on the main subdisciplines describe some vagaries associated with some of the anthropology subfields. Many of these chapters mention that journal prestige and reputation are especially important. Editors of highly selective journals have a wide selection of articles submitted to them. The editors and reviewers deem the most important and significant worthy of publishing. Other system checks exist—your thesis or dissertation committee and the imprimatur of university presses, to name two other gatekeepers—but you will be hard-pressed to duplicate the validation that comes from elite scholarly journals.

Second, publishing provides a public record of ideas. Publication documents you as the originator of specific contributions to the anthropological discourse. Some people refer to publishing as a formal registration of your ideas (see chapter 14 on copyright). Publishing thus makes your research visible and simultaneously facilitates ongoing credit to you. Robert Merton (1910–2003) produced fascinating scholarship on the sociology of knowledge, which, because he published, I can cite. In the 1600s, there were spectacular disputes over "simultaneous discovery," such as when Isaac Newton and Gottfried Leibniz both independently arrived at the conclusions that underlie differential calculus and each wished to crown himself the discoverer. Over the next centuries, these types of conflagrations decreased. Merton credits the modern scholarly journal as the mechanism that allowed authors to document their contributions publically, thus nearly eliminating contentious quarrels over whose work receives precedence.

In addition to these two benefits, I offer a final, third reason to publish. Merton's 1965 title, *On the Shoulder of Giants*, draws upon an oft-cited epigraph from a letter written by Newton: "If I have seen further it is only by standing on the shoulders of giants." Virtually every scholar I have met agrees that publication is an obligation of scholarship, that sharing one's thoughts, allowing others to build on them, and thus elevating the efforts of subsequent thinkers is a moral imperative. Anthropologists share this duty to enrich the discourse and increase collective understanding about humanity.

WHAT IS "PUBLISHING"?

I now turn to a harder question. Technology has begun to marvelously transform publishing, and so my fixed words attempt to circumscribe a rapidly moving target.

Publishing simply means making something public. When there were few technologies for duplicating copies and equally few mechanisms for distributing one's works, publishing remained a clear-cut activity. Documents were handwritten for private communication (i.e., "not published") or typeset and made public for others to read (i.e., "published"). This straightforward state of affairs continued for some 400 years. By the year 2010, the Internet, guided user interfaces, and software facilitated the ability of anyone with a computer and an Internet hookup to dispatch a wide range of content (written, visual, and audio) to the digital masses. If publishing is making something public, today any commenter on Facebook or poster to a blog is a publisher.

However, this book focuses on publishing that plays a role in your ability to secure a job and have a career as an anthropologist. While publishing undeniably includes making any text available on the Internet, not all content online will credential your ideas or ensure that credit returns to you. For your efforts to count as scholarly discourse, someone has to select and sanction your efforts by agreeing that your ideas are complete, your thoughts original, and your conclusions valid. In addition, not all digital activities support your means to claim authorship—today or in the future. In order for your contributions to count, you need to be able to derive recognition for your specific intellectual contribution, and others need to be able to cite your idea. Reliable citations require that text be fixed in specific versions and that future scholars be able to locate and read those fixed versions. Thus, archival arrangements and perpetual hosting must support the infrastructure that houses your contribution, or scholars may lose the ability to locate your contribution. An endeavor like Wikipedia is publishing in the generic sense, but I would not consider such articles to be scholarly publications because there has been no validation of the words, its contents are labile, and no credit is returned to authors for their specific contributions.

Scholarly publishing also means disseminating information beyond a private community of readers. Because this level of exposure entails more risks than sharing a paper in a seminar or your advisor's perusal of a draft, you usually hone the document before you place it before the public. A scholarly publisher, university press, or journal publisher will typically involve experts to improve your words and their presentation, such as sharing reviewer comments with you, copyediting your prose, and typesetting or otherwise formalizing the manuscript. Thus scholarly publishing also signifies a level of completeness in your work.

WHAT IS "PRIOR PUBLICATION"?

"Prior publication" in the humanities and social sciences is not as freighted as in the biomedical sciences, and this section will not apply to all anthropologists. This discussion may provide the most helpful guidance to anthropologists intending to publish in medical journals or some of the biological fields.

All journals require that authors sign agreements stipulating that the materials have not been previously published, and the author contracts of all prestigious publishing houses require that a work be "original" and not previously published. As making work public has become simpler—for instance with the ability for anyone to post documents on websites or to upload content to preprint servers and repositories—what constitutes "prior publication" becomes more elusive.

Journals

Journal editorial boards, particularly in the medical sciences, articulate the most explicit definitions of prior publication. These titles compete for original submissions, and their editors want to focus their reviewing efforts on hitherto unknown findings. There are typically four criteria for prior publication: (1) completeness of the earlier version, (2) validation, (3) public availability, and (4) the author's ability to transfer copyright. Some journals, such as the *Proceedings of the National Academy of Sciences*, incorporate combinations of these concepts.

In cases where prior publication looks at completeness, journals evaluate whether aspects of your article will still be novel to their readers. Thus, prior write-ups that shared results in detail may be considered previously published. *Focus: The Journal for Lifelong Learning in Psychiatry*, the *Journal of Human Evolution*, and the *Journal of Refractive Surgery* each allow publication of a brief abstract (fewer than 250 or 400 words, for instance). *Chest* explains that the key question is whether "the major elements of the study" were released earlier. The *American Journal of Veterinary Research* indicates that the editor will reject as previously published abstracts that included figures and illustrations, references, or details of the experimental design.

For other journals, the key determinant hinges on the revision process. These policies probe whether previous versions have been peer reviewed. For instance, the American Psychological Association's (APA) "Statement on PsychEXTRA, Prior Publication, and APA Journals" explains that a work changes significantly as a result of peer review, and thus task force reports and conference papers are eligible for journal consideration because they have not yet been peer reviewed and revised.

Some journals deem prior publication based on wide availability. These journals warn that "posting a manuscript on a host computer to which anyone on the Internet can gain access constitutes prior publication" (*Scandinavian Journal of Education Research*), and that "materials posted on the Internet or disseminated in other electronic form constitutes prior publication" (*American Journal of Managed Care*). *Chest*'s guidance to recent graduates affirms the need to circulate preprints and to post drafts online but suggests "authors avoid actively attracting a wider audience."

A final standard of prior publication examines whether the author controls the copyright. For instance, the Ecological Society of America indicates that "a necessary test for prior publication is whether the author can legally transfer copyright."

In the humanities and social sciences, journals also seek original thought and new ideas. The guidelines of many anthropology journals indicate that a work for consideration should not be previously published. Authors are asked to disclose any such prior publication, and editors evaluate situations on a case-by-case basis.

Dissertations and Book-Length Works

Increasingly, research institutions require that matriculating students deposit theses and dissertations into their campus's electronic libraries or repositories. Such requirements extend the long-standing tradition that students provide print copies so that the graduate school may own a complete archive of the works that formed the basis of granted degrees. The print availability of a single dissertation copy in one library's collection does not signify prior publication, but one electronic copy available to all digital denizens potentially means something different. As Colin Day, former director of the University of Michigan Press, wrote, "the degree of availability matters. If you have chosen to restrict access to people on the Virginia Tech campus, this will matter little to the publisher. But if you have allowed world-wide accessibility, then a publisher might well be concerned." Similarly, some graduate departments and programs have arrangements with UMI (University Microfilms International) that all students make their dissertations available in the ProQuest Dissertations and Theses database.

Students need to read the fine print carefully when they submit their works to UMI/ProQuest and to their institutional libraries or repositories. They should understand what is required, what dissemination options are available, and what rights as authors they retain. As a general rule, it is best to restrict access unless you have no plans to create further works from that same data. This is sadly because book publishing costs are high and sales of scholarly monographs are small. Thus, easy availability of a portion of a proposed book could undermine the incentives—which are extremely thin at most university presses under the best of circumstances—for a press to accept your project for publication. This point is rather plainly stated by Oxford University Press (OUP) in some tips:

> If you hope to publish your dissertation as a book, do not agree to its inclusion in an institutional or commercial online repository. Online delivery is an increasingly significant way of disseminating academic monographs and OUP could not take on a book substantially based on a dissertation already available online.

If you choose to follow this advice, you can complete all available metadata fields (title, subtitle, author, description of work, and keywords) and indicate that you would like the full-text manuscript embargoed. These descriptions will aid others in discovering the existence of your research, without compromising future publishing possibilities.

If you have not embargoed your thesis, take heart. The expectation at scholarly presses is that dissertations will be heavily revised—and editors mostly mean dramatically shortened. Thus, any book under contract will be "original" in the sense that you will completely retool your manuscript. Said differently, you can publish an original monograph derived from the research you published in your dissertation without any difficulty.

CONCLUSION

The dimensions of publishing have grown since Newton lived, and the technologies feeding the giant of scholarly publishing have changed since Newton's day, causing real transformations in what constitutes publishing and what is understood to be prior publication. Rapid advances of the Internet will lead to continued evolution of these concepts.

But some things have not changed since Newton wrote his famous letter. The fundamental value of scholarship and the advantages to those who participate in scholarly publishing continue. As technology improves and facilitates the dissemination of content, it increases the importance of knowing what others have said before you, of receiving validation and praise for your ideas, and of adding to the anthropological known world.

FURTHER READING

American Geophysical Union Council. "Policy on Dual or Prior Publication." First adopted by the council 20 April 1969, most recently revised 13 December 2009. http://www.agu.org/pubs/authors/policies/dualpub_policy.shtml, accessed April 1, 2011.

American Psychological Association Publications and Communications Board. "Statement on PsychEXTRA, Prior Publication, and APA Journals." Adopted November 2003. http://www.apa.org/pubs/databases/psycextra/statement.aspx, accessed April 1, 2011.

Day, Colin. "Guidance for Students Curious about Placing ETDs in a Digital Library Available to the Web." Published 16 December 1997, last modified 25 June 2008. http://www.ndltd.org/resources/publishers/guidance-for-students-curious-about-placing-etds-in-a-digital-library-available-to-the-web, accessed April 1, 2011.

Ecological Society of America. "Conditions for Manuscript Publication." Revised 18 February 2010. http://esapubs.org/esapubs/conditions.htm, accessed April 1, 2011.

Editorial Board. "PNAS Policy on Prior Publication." *Proceedings of the National Academy of Sciences (PNAS)* 96 (2009): 4215.

Frost, Charlotte. "Publisher Tips: Oxford University Press." 28 July 2010. http://www.phd2published.com/2010/07/28/publisher-tips-oxford-university-press/, accessed April 1, 2011.

IEEE/ACM Transactions on Networking. "Submissions." http://www.ton.seas.upenn.edu/submissions.html, accessed April 1, 2011.

Kaye, Sharon. "Why Publish?" *Academe* (American Association of University Professors), May/June 2008. http://www.aaup.org/AAUP/pubsres/academe/2008/MJ/Feat/kaye.htm, accessed April 1, 2011.

Langdon-Neuner, Elise. "When Does Previous Disclosure Become a 'Prior Publication' Problem?" *Chest* 135 (2009): 233. doi:10.1378/Chest.08-1255.

Merton, Robert K. *On the Shoulders of Giants.* Chicago: University of Chicago Press, 1965.

Scandinavian Journal of Education Research. "Instructions for Authors." http://www.tandf.co.uk/journals/journal.asp?issn=0031-3831&linktype=44, accessed April 1, 2011.

Soffer, Alfred. "What Constitutes Prior Publication?" *Chest* 92 (1987): 2. doi:10.1378/Chest.92.1.2.

Part I

STEP-BY-STEP GUIDANCE AND ADVICE

1

Attending Conferences and Organizing a Panel

Jason E. Miller

Anthropology students and young professionals can find the process of disseminating research findings to be challenging and a bit confusing. How do you get your work out there? Where is "there" anyway? This chapter offers practical advice about one of the best ways to share your work with others: attending and presenting your ideas at conferences.

Conferences are an ideal first step for several reasons. First, conference presentations generally do not constitute *publication*, because comments are oral and not widely circulated. (There are some notable exceptions, such as conferences where acceptance includes publication in the papers of the conference. For instance, if you present at the American Association of Physical Anthropologists, your paper will be published in the annual meeting supplement of the society's journal.) This advantage may seem counterintuitive in a book about publishing, but because your work is not printed, you still have time to retool, to revise, and make your work the best it can be without worrying that it is forever a part of the "literature." Second, conferences offer immediate feedback. Most conference attendees are supportive and offer both positive and constructive responses. Even if comments are less than glowing, they can still help you develop your ideas and improve your chances for acceptance in a later publication. Third, conferences serve as a way of formally registering your ideas. This means that you can list conference presentations on your curriculum vitae (your academic resume, often known as your "C.V.") as a preliminary registration of your idea within the structure of academe even though the conference paper or poster itself may not constitute a publication. Finally, conference attendance allows for in-person networking, which can be very useful in meeting editors, publishers, and other gatekeepers so that your work is seen by a wider audience.

This chapter explores how to choose a conference at which to share your work, different types of presentations at conferences, and how to organize a panel. It focuses on the largest American anthropology conferences including the annual meetings of the American Anthropological Association, the Society for Applied Anthropology, the Society for American Archaeology, and the American Association of Physical Anthropologists. However, many of the tips and suggestions are transferrable to other academic conferences.

CHOOSING A CONFERENCE

Anthropology conferences come in all shapes and sizes. One of the largest international conferences is the annual meeting of the American Anthropological Association (AAA), which averages over 500 concurrent sessions and 3,500 presenters each year. Other large anthropology conferences include the biennial World Congress of the International Union of Anthropological and Ethnological Sciences and the World Archaeological Congress. On a smaller scale, over 3,000 people attend the annual meeting of the Society for American Archaeology (SAA); the Society for Applied Anthropology (SfAA) draws attendance of usually about 1,200 anthropologists; and the American Association for Physical Anthropology (AAPA) represents another more targeted audience. Even more intimate, scores of specialized meetings attract a few hundred or a few handfuls of attendees, such as the Human Behavior and Evolution Society or the Society for Economic Anthropology. Also, regional conferences such as the Northwest Anthropology Conference or the Southern Anthropological Society often encourage student participation and have high acceptance rates. An additional bonus is that they are close to you so you can cut down on travel costs.

> **TIP:** Regional conferences can be a great place to present for the first time. Small audiences and high acceptance rates may translate to less fear for first-time presenters. AAA's website lists a calendar of meetings: http://www.aaanet.org.

Also, look for conferences that are not specifically for anthropologists but take place in a community-based setting or within related disciplines such as public health, education, history, or political science, as just a few examples. The holistic nature of anthropology lends itself to cross-disciplinary collaboration, and you never know who you might meet when you venture outside of anthropology.

When choosing a conference, consider how closely your work overlaps with the group sponsoring the conference. For example, if you study urban sprawl and development in Laos, you probably would not want to submit to a physical anthropology conference. While this may seem like common sense, many abstracts and panels get rejected for not matching the scope of a conference. Virtually all conferences have a "call for submissions" or "call for papers" that is posted on their websites. This call includes important information such as the date of the conference, the way in which submissions are accepted (e.g., mail or online submissions), and the format for submission (e.g., the number of words in the abstract). A lot of meeting websites include invaluable tips to help avoid rejection. Read the call for submissions closely. Panels are rejected for not following these guidelines exactly.

Many conference calls also include a theme for the conference. For example, the AAA and SfAA always have themes, whereas AAPA and SAA do not. These themes are developed by the conference organizers and are broad framing ideas around which the conference is organized. Some conferences require submitters to match the theme; it is optional in others. It is optional for both the AAA and the SfAA. Read the call and submission tips carefully to make sure your work is eligible to be accepted. Beyond this, some conferences, such as the AAPA conference, require that work submitted include results and analysis, while other conferences accept submissions that include more preliminary research plans or more reflexive, thought-based submissions.

TIP: The annual meetings of the AAA and SfAA always have a theme. Although you usually do not have to match the theme exactly, it is a good idea to incorporate some aspect of the theme into your panel if you are submitting an abstract to these conferences.

TYPES OF CONFERENCE PRESENTATIONS

Once you have selected a conference where you would like to present your work, the next step is deciding what kind of presentation you are going to give. In general, most conferences have two basic categories: papers and posters. For some meetings, these two different formats have different submission due dates. Papers are oral presentations (generally between 15 and 20 minutes in length) where a presenter will read a written paper or speak from prepared remarks. Increasingly, read papers are being replaced by presenters who follow PowerPoint presentations. Posters are large graphic displays.

Poster presenters arrive at a designated location and hour and set up their poster for a designated amount of time, such as two hours (for posters at the AAA and SAA) or three hours (AAPA and SfAA). Meeting attendees are free to walk around the room visiting the posters that interest them.

When deciding whether to submit a paper or poster, consider the advantages and challenges of each. Across most of anthropology, papers are seen as the traditional format for conference presentations, although posters have grown in popularity and respect over the past few years. In some subfields, namely biological anthropology, posters are seen as superior in some ways because they allow the author to include detailed data tables and information.

In general, paper panels are more formal than posters. Several presenters (up to 14 presenters at an AAPA symposium) each speak for their allotted time, and questions are held to the end of the session (assuming the session doesn't go over its allotted time!). Often, each session may only have time to answer one or two questions before the next session begins. Some audience members may approach presenters after comments to ask follow-up questions or to ask for a copy of the presentation. The paper format does not always allow for much interaction between audience and presenter. In contrast, poster presentations are highly interactive. Viewers are much more likely to ask questions of presenters or give feedback. This can be a wonderful opportunity to gain ideas for improving your research or to network with others who are engaged in similar areas. Beyond gaining more feedback, many first-time presenters find the idea of reading a formal paper to be a bit intimidating. A poster presenter need only interact with one or two people at a time, in a more conversational style. In addition, posters lend themselves to work that is more visual in nature.

Both papers and posters are grouped together in panels. Confusingly, conferences use different names for panels and have different requirements for the number of participants. Various types of panels can carry a different level of prestige and "weight" on your curriculum vitae. At both the AAA and SAA annual meetings, the most prestigious panels are referred to as "invited panels" or "sponsored symposia," meaning the presenters have been invited to participate in the meeting. These panels are organized in advance and go through the formal review process before the deadline for submission. These panels then get to bypass the review process after the submission deadline because, in effect, they are accepted before they are submitted.

Many novices believe one must be a senior anthropologist to receive invited status, but this isn't true. Anyone can contact the program chair to pitch an idea for an invited session. If the program chair likes your idea, believes it fits in well with the theme of the conference, and believes that your proposed panel will be of interest to members of the association or section, your odds of being invited are high. The AAPA has a similar type of special-status panel referred to as a "symposium." These sessions have up to 14 presenters and are arranged in advance in consultation with the program chair. Not all conferences have invited panels, and some conferences have even more prestigious sessions called "executive panels" or "special panels." At the SfAA, the highest level of panel is referred to as a "plenary session" and is organized directly by the program chair. Consult the conference's call for papers for more information on these special types of panels.

TIP: Anyone can organize an invited panel at the AAA meeting or a symposium at the AAPA. Contact the meeting or program chair and discuss your ideas—you have nothing to lose and a lot to gain!

Beyond invited panels, the average conference panel is referred to as "volunteered" (AAA), a "session" (SAA) or "regular panel" or poster (SfAA), or a "podium session" or poster (AAPA). For these panels, the panel organizer coordinates finding individuals who will present papers or posters that are similar to the organizer's. The organizer creates a session title and abstract that speaks to the collection and submits this panel title and abstract along with the titles and abstracts of the individual papers or posters in the session. The size of these panels varies by conference. The SfAA has 5 papers per panel, and SAA allows up to 16 papers per symposium. These panel submissions are then reviewed by the program committee for possible inclusion. Posters are also grouped into sessions and scheduled as sessions throughout the run of the conference at the AAA, SAA, and AAPA. The SfAA has one large poster session containing all posters in one place at one time.

There may be different due dates for different types of submissions. Be sure to check the call for papers to see when different types of submissions (such as invited sessions, contributed sessions, or forums) are due.

The poster and podium sessions of the AAPA are different from other conferences in that they are not organized by the presenters (meaning that individuals do not organize nonsymposia panels) but are put together from individually volunteered poster or paper submissions around set themes by the program committee after the submission deadline. The other three conferences also have this type of panel, which is constructed by the program committee itself. These panels are composed of individually volunteered papers or posters that were not submitted as part of an organized session. Sometimes colloquially referred to as "orphans" by the AAA, the program committee attempts to group strong individually volunteered submissions together and create panels. SAA refers to these panels as "contributed panels," and the AAA calls them "volunteered panels." SfAA and AAPA cluster many presentations this way. The SAA distinguishes between "contributed papers" (which address problems of theory, method, history, and progress) and "research reports" (recent field-based research). In general, it is not noticeable on the final conference program which panels are composed of individually volunteered papers and which were organized.

ORGANIZING A PANEL

At this point, you have decided which conference you would like to present your work at, and you may have decided to organize a panel. One of the best, albeit costly, ways to begin this process is to attend the conference before attempting to be a presenter. By attending you can get a feel for what the conference is like and what kinds of research and presentations are accepted. Attending a conference also allows you to meet others who have similar research interests. Since one of the jobs of a panel organizer is to find other presenters for their panel, this networking can be extremely valuable. A lot of planning goes on at the current year's conference for next year's meeting. If you can't attend a conference before presenting the next year, don't despair; there are other ways to organize a panel.

Program Chairs Are Your Friends

Every conference has a program chair. These individuals are responsible for coordinating the conference and also for the selection process. The AAA, AAPA, SAA, and SfAA have a primary conference program chair(s) and a program committee. The AAA, SAA, and SfAA also comprise smaller groups (variously referred to as sections, interest groups, committees, or TIGs [topical interest groups]), and each of these groups organizes time on the program as well. The AAPA also has smaller groups who organize panels around set themes for the conference. Every section of the AAA (such as the Society for Visual Anthropology or the National Association for the Practice of Anthropology) has its own program chair and program committee. The committees and interest groups of the SAA and SfAA organize specific aspects of these section programs.

Rather than pitching your idea to the main conference program chair, try contacting the program chair of the section(s) that most overlaps with your research interests. The section program chair(s) can help you identify others who may be interested in being on your panel and provide suggestions and critiques to help ensure that your panel is accepted. Be sure to do this as early as possible. Sections, TIGs, and committees have a limited amount of time on the program (perhaps only one session), and commitments fill up fast. Most program chairs want to help, and they may guide or fine-tune your submission ahead of time. If they have doubts about your panel, it is better to know that ahead of time. It is never too soon to start talking to a program chair about your idea.

Where to Submit?

Some conferences (AAA and AAPA) will ask submitters to list a section or interest group to review your panel submission. Some conferences (AAPA) have a review committee that looks at submissions by particular committees. Other conferences (SAA and SfAA) will only offer general review by one large committee. For conferences that have sections or interest groups, think about what section would be the best reviewer for your panel.

At the AAA, each section gets a certain amount of time on the conference program to fill as it sees fit based on the number of people who are members of the section. The more people who belong to a section, the more time slots it gets. You might think this means you're better off submitting your panel to a large section. However, large sections (such as the General Anthropology Division or the Society for Cultural Anthropology) get hundreds of submissions each year and are responsible for programming to a wide audience. Smaller sections may have less time on the program, but they also have fewer members and their focus is much tighter. Try to find a section compatible with your own research, and contact the section's program chair months before the deadline to discuss the possibilities of organizing a panel. Remember that you may need to be a member of a section if you wish to make a proposal for a panel. Ask the section's program chair if this is the case.

Another excellent option for students is to submit a panel to the National Association of Student Anthropologists (NASA). NASA is a large section of the AAA that serves students and helps them organize panels for the conference. NASA's large number of members translates to a sizeable amount of time on the annual meeting program—time specifically set aside for students and panels of interest to students. (Not all presenters on NASA's program are students; for example, there have been several panels in the past that are designed to connect students and new professionals with "big names" in anthropology or other senior anthropologists.) The NASA program committee gladly assists students in helping to organize their panels and often accommodates most of the submissions they review, leading to a comparably low rejection rate for panels. NASA also organizes annual panels of volunteered papers and posters specifically for undergraduate students.

Writing a Panel Abstract and Seeking Participants

Once you have gotten some feedback on your idea, it is time to begin writing the title and abstract for your panel. Your panel title and abstract should be specific enough to let audience members know what your panel is about while being general enough to include all panelists' papers as a cohesive group. The title of your panel will be the first (and possibly only) thing prospective audience members will read. Academics love panels that inject a little bit of humor or wit, but remember, you are not applying to be a standup comic. There is a fine line between a witty title that piques audience interest and an amateurish joke that weakens your credibility as an anthropologist.

When writing an abstract, read the directions in the call for papers closely. When a call says an abstract is limited to a certain number of words, it means it. An otherwise great panel might be rejected for not following the guidelines. Since you have a limited number of words, make them count. Include information on what audience members can expect if they come to your panel and also justify briefly why your panel is important to other anthropologists. Avoid jargon. Also, remember that your abstract is your chance to tell the program committee why your panel deserves to be on the program. Have a few people read your draft to make sure the abstract sounds as good to others as it sounds to you. Ask your readers whether they can tell you what your panel is about in their own words. If they cannot, it is time to revise. You can also send a draft of your abstract and title to a program chair and ask for feedback.

> **TIP:** When writing an abstract, be sure to limit the amount of jargon you use. Think of the abstract as a way to market your panel. What can you say about your panel that will attract prospective audience members and make them want to attend?

You may have gotten some leads for panel participants from attending other meetings, from your advisor, or by connecting with other students. But for students at smaller departments or for those who haven't been to conferences, you may need to post to listservs in your subdiscipline in order to locate other papers for your conference. If someone has already posted a similar call, why not join forces and work together? AAA has a bulletin board, and every February and March it is filled with people looking for panelists. Anyone can post on the bulletin board. Other meetings similarly have boards and listservs to help panel organizers.

Process after Submission

After you have submitted your panel, your information will be forwarded to the program committee for review. Several individuals will rank your submission against others to see whether it warrants inclusion in the program. For example, two members of the AAPA program committee review each submission. If they suggest that a submission be rejected, an additional third reviewer reviews it. The SAA and SfAA use a similar process. The process for the AAA is somewhat more complex. Your submission is routed to the program chair for the section that you selected during the submission process. If you secured invited status for your panel ahead of time, your session is approved and it is on the program. If you did not receive invited status, the section program committee ranks each submission and groups volunteered papers and posters into sessions. Finally, all of the section's recommendations are forwarded to the AAA program committee, which makes the ultimate decision using the section's ranked lists.

Program committees look for various things when deciding whether to accept a panel, including whether the panel is complete (e.g., whether it is full and all members have submitted their titles, abstracts, and registrations in the correct way); how closely it matches the theme and scope of the conference; how strong the abstracts and titles appear; and how many people might attend the panel at the conference. In a few months, the panel organizer and sometimes all of the panelists will be contacted by the program chair and told whether their panel has been accepted.

FINAL THOUGHTS

In closing, remember that organizing a panel and presenting at an academic conference are not nearly as scary as they may seem. Be confident in your ability and in your research and have fun. If you are rejected, don't focus on the rejection, but focus on how you can improve to make another attempt. Find a different conference or section and try again.

RESOURCES

American Anthropological Association
http://www.aaanet.org
American Association of Physical Anthropologists
http://www.physanth.org

Human Behavior and Evolution Society
  http://hbes.com
National Association for Student Anthropologists
  http://www.aaanet.org/sections/nasa
Northwest Anthropological Association
  http://www.class.uidaho.edu/nwaa
Society for American Archaeology
  http://www.saa.org
Society for Applied Anthropology
  http://www.sfaa.org
Society for Economic Anthropology
  https://seawiki.wikidot.com
Southern Anthropological Society
  http://southernanthro.org
World Archaeological Congress
  http://www.worldarchaeologicalcongress.org
World Congress of the International Union of Anthropological and Ethnological Sciences
  http://wcaanet.org/member/iuaes

2

Creating and Presenting an Academic Poster

John K. Trainor

Do you want a way to share your research findings with a wide audience visually rather than orally? If so, then you might think about making an academic poster to present your research.

Posters are not for everyone and every research project, but the poster should not be dismissed out of hand. First, the poster is the preferred method of sharing your research in some subfields (such as physical anthropology and archaeology) and is growing in popularity and importance among cultural and linguistic anthropologists, particularly those offering visual evidence. There are many pros and cons to using the poster format to present your research. Posters allow for greater interaction and networking with people while avoiding the feeling of being on stage or under a spotlight. Posters often make your research more accessible as people can quickly get the main ideas and then follow up with questions. Posters can even give you the chance to win money in competitions and add a line to your C.V. or resume.

> **TIP:** If you are a student, there can be added incentives to using the poster format: many anthropology associations, including the American Association of Physical Anthropologists, the Society for American Archaeology, and the Society for Applied Anthropology, have student poster competitions. Winning these competitions will not only look good on your C.V. (or resume), but some of these competitions also offer cash prizes.

There are, of course, drawbacks to the poster format as well. These drawbacks include the fact that some groups still view the poster as inferior to a paper, posters are inherently visual and not all research is best described visually, posters require that the final version of your presentation be done well in advance of your presentation, and poster printing can be expensive (see the "Printing Your Poster" section for tips on how to make poster printing more affordable). All of these benefits and barriers must be weighed before you decide which format is best for presenting your research.

The old adage is that a picture is worth a thousand words, and in cases where you have compelling photographs, posters can be a terrific way of effectively demonstrating your case. Don't be quick to assume that your methods and results are not visual. Often maps, GIS (geographic information system) data, social networks, and other contextual data can be conveyed in eye-catching ways. As well, anthropologists who are very green (ones who have never been to a meeting before) or shy and uncertain speakers may find a poster session one of the easiest and least intimidating ways to get a toe into the waters and receive preliminary feedback on their ideas. A poster may be the easiest way to get invited status and can often increase your chances of acceptance in general (see table 2.1).

If your work is theoretical or your content is highly abstract, the poster is not for you. If you are hitting the job market that year, in many instances you would be wiser to think in terms of a paper presentation, because members of your search committee may desire to "see you in action." Table 2.1 may help you decide whether the poster is right for your research project.

HOW TO MAKE A POSTER

You've decided that the poster format is the best way to present your research, so what is the next step? Before you can begin you have to decide what computer program you want to use to create your poster. There is no short supply of programs available; you can use Microsoft PowerPoint, Microsoft Publisher, Adobe InDesign, or many others. I discuss how to make a poster in PowerPoint as many are familiar with this easy-to-use program and have it on their computers. PowerPoint is by no means the most powerful design software, and if you have the skills and access to use another design program, the same guidelines will apply.

POSTER SETUP

Before you start designing your poster you need to set up the poster in the program you are using. This is a very important step. If you begin making your poster before you set the size, you will quickly find that there is not enough room and your background and pictures may not be of high enough quality when you enlarge your poster. To set your page size in PowerPoint,

Table 2.1. Is the Poster Format for You?

Benefits of Posters	*Disadvantages to Posters*
Greater interaction and networking with people.	Posters require brevity; you need to be able to concisely express your main points.
Visuals may be easier to quickly understand and attract attention.	Printing requires advance planning. There is no last-minute tweaking just before you present.
Visual format allows for more creativity.	Poster printing can be expensive, especially on a short turnaround time.
Many conferences have student poster competitions that come with cash prizes.	Not all subdisciplines (or even sections/interest areas) value a poster as much as a paper.
Presenting a poster can be less intimidating—no standing on a "stage" in front of a large crowd.	

you need to find "Page Setup." In Macintosh versions of PowerPoint, this can be found under the File menu, Page Setup submenu. In newer Windows versions, this can be found on the design tab of the ribbon. Under Page Setup, there are two important settings to adjust: page size (height and width) and orientation.

Page size is key to a successful poster. You don't want your poster to be too small (even though it will be cheaper to print), as it will be hard to read from afar, but you also don't want your poster to be so big that it doesn't fit in the space allotted. There is not one standard size for posters—this varies by conference and can be found on the meeting's website. If you are unable to find listed measurements for poster size, a good rule of thumb is 3 feet by 4 feet (you can start with this size while waiting to hear back from conference planners about their particular size requirements). Websites might not list a required size, but they will more often than not give you the dimensions of the board or table space you will have while presenting. You should never go over your allotted space, as you may encroach on others' posters or have your poster curl in on itself, thus obstructing the content you worked so hard to create, or you may even be asked to take your poster down.

TIP: If you are entering a student poster competition, many require that your poster meet, but not exceed, size guidelines to be eligible. Also, printing posters is an investment, and you are wiser to make sure what dimensions you want before you send your files to a printer. If there is any doubt, contact conference planners and be sure your poster meets eligibility requirements.

Also, at this point you will need to choose the orientation of your poster, be it portrait or landscape. The most common orientation is landscape and most backgrounds you find will be in this format, but I have seen some innovative posters that are in portrait orientation.

POSTER BACKGROUND

Next, I recommend choosing a background. While you can continue to construct your poster without a background, backgrounds often limit your space and will dictate where things are placed. For these reasons, choose your background before you start adding text, images, and figures. Where can you find a poster background? First, if you are presenting information that was obtained using grant funds or with a research center, verify whether they have a required background. Your university, research center, museum, or laboratory where you research may have a design you can choose to use. In all these cases, the granting agency or your employer's imprimatur can lend an aura of credibility to your work, and I recommend you consider opting for one of these backgrounds. However, you may have free rein to select your own background. If so, opt for a light neutral color.

There are also many websites where you can download premade PowerPoint templates. One place to start looking is directly at Microsoft (http://office.microsoft.com/en-us/templates). You can find premade templates online, but not all are free. And, as with downloading anything from the Internet, use only trusted resources to avoid malicious code that can harm your computer. If you make your own background or download one from the Internet, I strongly recommend choosing a conservative background. A background full of pictures or with wild colors can be distracting and hard to read. Let your creativity shine in other areas of poster design such as layout, image content, and even content.

POSTER CONTENT

As a rule of thumb, your poster should include anything you would have said in an oral presentation, although generally your comments will be in less depth. Virtually all posters have these sections: introduction, methods, results, conclusions, and works cited/acknowledgments. Some conferences mandate what sections are required for your poster, such as an abstract, so be sure to look at any guidelines provided by conference planners. Knowing the sections will help you get started thinking of your poster just as you would a written paper, but remember to keep your words to a minimum. Often the best way to present material on a poster is in bulleted lists or to set certain key words in boldface. You may choose to use only paragraph form in your introduction and conclusion sections, which often do not lend themselves to bullet statements.

It is not easy to limit your words, and there is no absolute rule about how much text should be on your poster. Try to limit yourself to five pages in a 20-point font in the text editing software of your choice. It may seem hard to limit your text, but remember that the poster format is an interactive format. You do not need to include every detail; use your text, images, and figures to paint a broad picture. People who are interested will take the time to ask you questions to learn more. If you try to include everything in your poster, it will be too text heavy, and people may not even stop to read your poster, feeling it is "too much."

Always type your content in a text-editing program (like Microsoft Word) and not into the poster itself. This will make it much easier to catch typos and to edit and revise your content. Just like any paper, you should revise, revise, and revise before you print the final version. Solicit a friend who knows relatively little about your topic to read the text and confirm that the information reads clearly. After you are happy with your text, you can copy and paste it into your poster. Always proofread one final time in the poster format to be sure you did not miss any mistakes and that there were no problems while copying and pasting.

In addition to your text, obviously the most important part of the poster is the role of the visual elements. Illustrations can include photos that contextualize your data, physical maps, maps of social networks, charts, graphs, or anything else that you think expresses your point. Title and caption your visual elements (i.e., "Figure 1") so that you can reference them within the text with ease. Just as with the background, you need to be aware of the resolution of any image you use. Images at a low resolution will look blocky or pixilated when enlarged for your poster.

TIP: Generally images with a resolution of 300 dpi should be suitable to print on a 3′ × 4′ poster. Always zoom to 100% to verify that all images look the way you want them to when enlarged.

HOW TO LAY OUT YOUR POSTER

You do not need to be an artist to make a visually appealing poster. There are a few simple design rules that can ensure your poster is attractive and has good flow. First and foremost, be judicious with your words. The poster should be organized in such a way that images are as close to related text as possible. Don't refer in your introduction to a demographics chart that is located at the end of your poster. When possible, call out visual elements in text just as you would in a journal article (e.g., "see figure 1"). This is critical to having a well-organized, clear poster.

You may be tempted to make your poster perfectly symmetrical. The "classic" poster design is a title bar across the top of the page with three or four columns that include text and images. There is nothing wrong with this design; it is the design I most commonly use, but don't be limited by it. Symmetry isn't required to have an attractive poster, but balance is. What is "balance"? Imagine you are making a poster and you place a large image or chart on the upper right corner of your poster. Without other images, your poster will look lopsided or out of balance. Now mentally add another picture to the lower left corner of this imaginary poster. Although not symmetrical, the poster is back in balance and pleasing to the eye.

In addition to balance, an important design rule is the "rule of thirds." The rule of thirds essentially states that the eye will follow a Z pattern across your poster. The most important elements of your poster should fall on this imaginary Z. For more in-depth discussion of the rule of thirds as applied to posters, go to "Creating Anthropology Conference Posters" on the AAA website (see "Further Reading"). This PDF explains design principles in detail.

Finally, remember the importance of "white space." White space does not actually have to be white, but it should be free of images and text. The proper use of white space keeps your poster from feeling crowded and helps it to flow. Critical areas for white space include the border of your poster (try to reserve at least an inch on all sides of your poster) as well as around every textbox and visual element. How much white space you leave will be dictated by your design and how much information you include on your poster. Do not try to cheat by cutting white space and including more text—this will make for a less appealing, less readable poster. Remember, if your poster doesn't catch someone's eye or if it overwhelms the viewer with text, no one will stop to look at it.

THE NUTS AND BOLTS OF POSTER MAKING

At this point you should have your PowerPoint sized, a background selected, and your text written (and revised!) in another program. Here are a few key design rules to guide you in creating your poster. Remember any useful tips and tricks you may have from putting together presentations in PowerPoint in the past, as many apply to poster making. The most basic, and critical, element you will use is the textbox. Everywhere you want to add text, you will need to add a textbox.

> **TIP:** Using multiple textboxes allows for flexibility, so don't use one large textbox for all your content. Poster presenters often use one textbox for each section of text. Also, any shape you use in PowerPoint can be turned into a textbox by right-clicking and selecting Add Text.

Textboxes have many options that you may use. There are many ways to find these options depending on which version of PowerPoint you are using, but in all versions you can get to textbox options by right-clicking on the textbox and selecting Format Textbox or Format Shape. The Fill option is essentially the textbox's background. The Fill option is also where you can set the transparency of the textbox. Fill and transparency are useful when you want your textbox to stand out from the background you have chosen. Another option for textboxes is Line. Line refers to whether or not you want a border around your textboxes and how thick (or heavy) you want the line to be. Finally, you can set alignment, margins, and columns in the Format pane. This may be easier than using the ribbon, formatting palette, or drop-down menus, depending on your version of PowerPoint.

Font is critical. As a rule of thumb, stick with standard, easy-to-read fonts such as Arial, Calibri, or Cambria. Even these fonts will be too hard to read if you use a smaller font size to try to squeeze in more content. Also, it is generally easiest to read dark fonts on a light background. Avoid using wild colors for text, although vivid colors can work well in graphics, such as to draw people's attention to a statistically significant result in a chart.

Regarding font size, the choice is ultimately yours, but here are some suggestions to get you started: titles should be at least 84-point font, section headings (e.g., "Introduction," "Conclusion") should be at least 48-point, and body text should be at least 24-point. Of these, the most critical is the body font size. If you try to squeeze more in by going below a 24-point font, people standing at a regular distance will not be able to read your poster. If space allows, consider using even larger font sizes for body text. Just be sure the font size is uniform across the poster, that is, one size for the title, one size for headings, and one size for body text. When in doubt, set the view to 100% and stand a few feet from your computer screen. If you can easily read the text, your font size is likely adequate.

As you add images and other visual elements, use PowerPoint to its fullest. There are features in PowerPoint that can enhance your images with ease. These functions include adding a border to your images, setting a color as transparent, or even using shadows and reflections. In newer versions of PowerPoint, all of these functions are available in the ribbon (or the formatting palette on a Mac) when you click on a picture; in older versions of PowerPoint, you can find them by right-clicking on the image. These functions can highlight your visual elements and items such as borders can help remind you to use white space wisely.

TIP: Make sure all groupings of text and images are in line with each other.

If text is not clearly grouped, it will be hard to read. I recommend starting with three columns of text using three large text boxes, as in figure 2.1. (Be sure to use PowerPoint's auto alignment feature.) As you start to add different elements, you can break these columns, but you always want to make sure the text has a clear, easy-to-read flow. Remember that rules are made to be broken, but the end result should always be neat and clear.

PRINTING YOUR POSTER

You have spent hours putting together a poster that is both informative and visually appealing, but printing is just as important. How your poster is printed can make or break the result. There are two limiting factors regarding where you can print your poster: time and size. Printing a poster is no small undertaking, and you should remember this as you begin to work on it. Unlike an oral presentation where you can fine-tune your PowerPoint slides minutes before your presentation, this is not the case with a poster. At a minimum, you will need 24 hours to get your poster printed, and a turnaround this fast may increase your costs significantly.

Businesses like FedEx Office (previously known as Kinko's), Office Max, and Office Depot will offer you the shortest turnaround time, but even these places may require 24 or 48 hours. Also, not all locations can print posters the size you will need. Unless cost is no issue, plan ahead to save money on printing. If you can have your poster done a month before you leave for a conference, you will have more economical choices. Call local printers, as they can often offer you a good deal. Most local printers will quote you a price by the square foot, so have a calculator handy and be ready to do a little math (for a 3′ × 4′ poster, you would multiply the square-foot price by the area of your poster, 12 feet). Also, know your measurements when you call the printers. Ask each printer how long printing will take, as not all printers

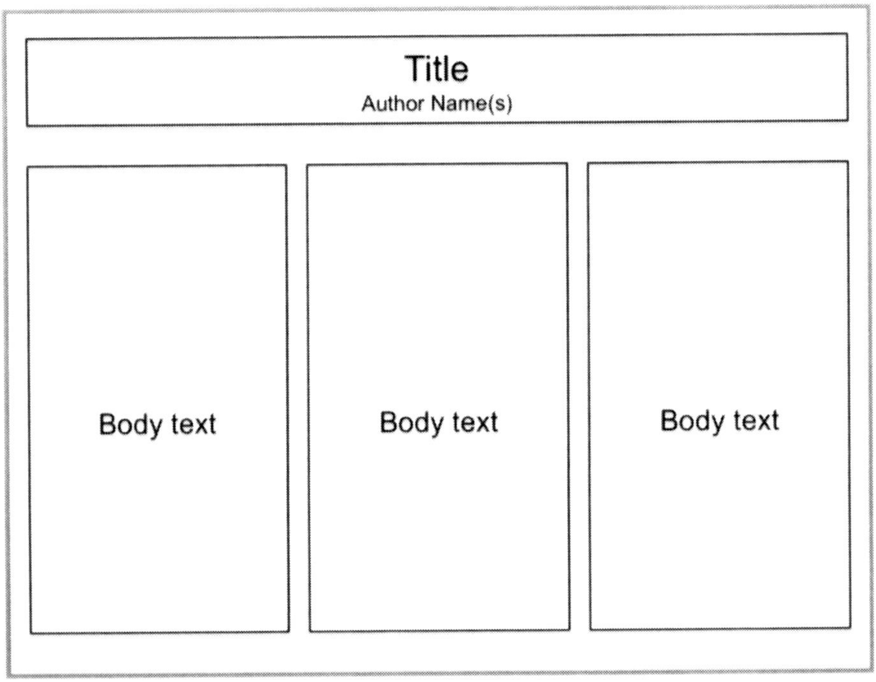

Figure 2.1. General poster layout. This basic layout can help you get started. While the textboxes in this sample have borders, this is just to show how the visual space should be filled. In general, textboxes with borders can be distracting unless used to clearly delineate sections of text. To help you see how much this format can be varied, I include a link to some award-winning life science posters in the "Resources" section of the chapter.

will produce your poster in house. You also may need to decide whether you want your poster printed on matte (flat) or glossy (shiny) paper.

If you are doing this ahead of time, check out the Internet. Many mail-order printing services offer good prices if you give them enough lead time to print and ship your poster.

Finally, your university may offer low-cost (or even free) poster printing. Places to find on-campus printing services include the computer store, science and engineering departments (where posters are the main method of presenting research), and even the library.

Poster printing can be a costly endeavor, and even if it is affordable, you only want to do it once. Ask colleagues and advisors where they have had their posters printed. They can help you find low-cost options and steer you away from places that are expensive or have low-quality printing services.

Once you have selected the printer for your poster, you need to get the digital file to them. I strongly recommend converting your PowerPoint to a PDF (portable document file) whenever possible. The printer may use a different operating system, a different version of PowerPoint, or even a different program to open and print the PowerPoint. All of these differences can alter your poster; using a PDF format allows for uniformity across platforms and programs. If you use Mac OS X, the PDF function is built into the save and print functions on your computer. On a Windows-based machine, you can use Adobe Professional or a free PDF writer such as CutePDF (see "Resources").

Finally, ask your printer to let you see a proof before printing; this is your last chance to find any errors. If your poster prints incorrectly due to something outside the printer's control (such as incompatibility between versions of PowerPoint), you will often have to pay for a reprint. Save time and money by seeing a proof when possible. While you're picking up your poster, buy a poster tube for transporting your work safely to the conference.

PRESENTING YOUR POSTER

Before you can present your poster, you will need to set it up. The time available to do this differs from conference to conference, but plan on being there approximately 20 minutes early. Supplies available to you will vary. In general, conferences supply a place to hang your poster (usually a poster board or a bulletin board/cubicle wall) as well as the tools required to hang your poster (usually pushpins). If you do not receive this information in your acceptance letter, search the conference website or contact planners in advance. Always check with the session chair or association staff before hanging your poster, as you may be assigned a specific space to hang your poster (some conference programs will indicate an assigned space number).

> **TIP:** You may want to bring some tape, pushpins, and other hanging supplies just to be prepared for any scenario.

The amount of time you have to present your poster varies by conference; it can range from two hours (AAA) to four hours (SfAA). Be prepared to stand by your poster the entire time; this means you should go to the bathroom before your poster session begins, and bring a bottle of water, as you may be talking for much of that time. While presenting your poster, people will often walk right by. Don't take offense, as no one's research will interest everyone. Some people will stop and ask you questions. Don't be nervous, as the majority will just be curious and friendly. It helps to have a one- or two-sentence spiel describing what you did and what you found. If people are still interested, they will then be able to ask you more in-depth questions.

It is fairly common to be asked for a copy of your poster. Be prepared with a printout of your poster—an affordable easy-to-read option is a black and white version on legal-size paper. Don't forget about the back. Use the back-side of your handout to list additional resources, show off a research tool you used, or add anything else you think is apropos. Include your name and e-mail on your handout. Also, bring a business card holder and some business cards to place next to your poster (if you have a table). If you don't have business cards, print some at home or find a website that offers free or low-cost printing such as VistaPrint (www.vistaprint.com).

The biggest benefit to presenting a poster is that you meet people one on one who do similar research. This is a critical time to network and can lead to information about jobs, future research partnerships, and other opportunities. Finally, if the presentation guidelines allow, bring your laptop. It can be an effective tool to showcase pictures, show off a web page related to your research (if web access is available), or even show a video related to your research. Be creative and use your time and space wisely.

CONCLUSION

A poster is a powerful tool to share your research. It allows for more intimate interaction with colleagues interested in your research and can allow for in-depth networking. Posters also allow you to be more creative, showcasing your research in a visual and more personal manner. While a poster requires more preparation time than a paper, it can be well worth the time and effort. Consider making a poster for your next conference.

FURTHER READING

Block, Stephen M. "Do's and Don'ts of Poster Presentations." *Biophysical Journal* 71, no. 3527 (December 1996). http://www.ncbi.nlm.nih.gov/pmc/articles/PMC1233841, accessed April 1, 2011.

Hess, George R. "Creating Effective Poster Presentations: Resources." Version 3, 2010. http://www.ncsu.edu/project/posters/NewSite/Resources.html, accessed April 1, 2011.

Maltby, Henderika J., and M. Serrell. "The Art of Poster Presentation." *Collegian: Journal of the Royal College of Nursing Australia* 5, no. 2 (1998): 36–37.

Miller, Jason E., and Trainor, John K. "Creating Anthropology Posters: A Guide for Beginners." 2007. http://www.aaanet.org/meetings/upload/How-to-Create-Anthropology-Posters.pdf, accessed April 1, 2011.

Miller, Lynne, et al. "Expanded Guidelines for Giving a Poster Presentation." Prepared for the American Society of Primatologists. https://www.asp.org/education/posterpresentationguidelines.cfm, accessed April 1, 2011.

RESOURCES

Cute PDF
 http://www.cutepdf.com

Poster Examples
 http://www.lib.umn.edu/undergrad/symposium/poster_gallery_04/index.phtml
 http://www.ncsu.edu/project/posters/NewSite/ExamplePosters.html

Poster Templates
 http://office.microsoft.com/en-us/templates

3

Presenting a Paper

Paul N. Edwards

We've all sat through poor presentations. The speaker approaches the head of the room and sits down at the table. (You can't see through the heads in front of you.) He begins to read from a paper, speaking in a soft monotone. (You can hardly hear. Soon you're nodding off.) Sentences are long, complex, and filled with jargon. The speaker emphasizes complicated details. (You rapidly lose the thread of the talk.) With five minutes left in the session, the speaker suddenly looks at his watch. He announces—in apparent surprise—that he will have to omit some important points because time is running out. He shuffles papers, becoming flustered and confused. (So do you, if you're still awake.) The speaker drones on. Fifteen minutes after the scheduled end of the talk, the host reminds the speaker to finish for the third time. The speaker trails off inconclusively and asks for questions. (Thin, polite applause finally rouses you from dreamland.)

Why do otherwise brilliant people give such soporific talks? For one thing, they're scared. The pattern is an understandable, if dysfunctional, reaction to stage fright. It's easier to hide behind the armor of a written paper—which they have had plenty of time to work through—than to simply stand up and talk.

But second, and much more important, it's part of academic culture—especially in the humanities and qualitative social sciences. It's embedded in our language: we say we're going to "give a paper." As a euphemism for a talk, that's an oxymoron. *Presentations are not journal articles.* They're a completely different medium of communication, and they require a different set of skills. Professors often fail to recognize this. Even more often they fail to teach it to their graduate students.

Everybody has to confront stage fright in his or her own way. But academic culture is something we can deliberately change. This chapter jump-starts that process with some pointers for conference presentations and effective public speaking.

WHAT PRESENTING IS ALL ABOUT

Listening is hard work. Especially at conferences, where audiences listen to many talks over many hours, people need the speaker's help to maintain their focus. Therefore, any effective speaker must do three things: communicate the arguments and evidence, persuade the audience that the arguments are sound, and, finally, interest and entertain.

In our obsession with persuasive arguments and evidence, academics too often forget about the third item in this list. Sometimes we think it follows automatically from the first two. (It doesn't.) Sometimes we even scoff at the goal itself. Some of us seem to believe that if a talk is entertaining or easy to follow, it's probably not very deep. Even more perversely, some of us believe that if a talk is dense and difficult to follow, it's profound and important.

These assumptions are false. It is impossible to communicate and persuade effectively without entertaining as well. Keeping people interested and involved—entertaining them—matters, because in order to communicate your work and its value, *you need listeners' full attention.* This is the true meaning and significance of "entertainment." In an academic talk, entertainment isn't about making your audience laugh or distracting them from their troubles—it's about keeping them focused on and interested in what you have to say.

As well, if you're giving an academic talk at a meeting where you'll also be interviewing for a job, you should assume that some of your potential colleagues will attend your talk. They will vet the presentation not only for what it indicates about your research, but also for insight into what kind of teacher you might be. Because the principles in this chapter address effective communication, they apply to presenting any kind of material, including front-of-class lessons. Finally, presenting your work at a conference can be a useful first step toward publishing research. An engaging, insightful presentation can help set the tone for a journal article down the road.

PREPARING YOUR TALK

Plan it out. Very likely your talk will be based on a paper. Even more likely, though, you won't have enough time to present everything you wrote. I strongly advise you against reading aloud, but it helps to know that even if you *do* read aloud, you won't be able to read more than about 1,500 words in a 15-minute presentation. (People talk at about 100 words per minute.) That's about six pages of double-spaced text. So your first step must be to plan, very carefully, exactly what you want to say.

That means you're going to have to choose. To do this, consider exactly what you want your audience to remember about your talk. In a 15-minute conference talk, you have time to make no more than one or two main points, and you won't be able to elaborate on them very much. In a 45-minute job interview, you can go considerably deeper, but you still won't have time to read an entire 6,000-word article aloud.

To start, briefly describe the purpose of your work (the problems you're trying to solve, the theories you're building or developing, an ethnographic base you're creating or extending, etc.).You will also need to say something about your field site and your methods. Keep this introductory part as brief as possible. Then select one or two main points, elaborating each one with a few pieces of supporting evidence. Finally, wrap it up with a very short summary, one you can deliver in one minute or less.

If you're basing your talk on a finished paper, it's very important to realize that you will have to cut large parts of it for the talk. The most common mistake in academic presentations is to try to cram everything in. *Don't do it.* Especially in a panel situation, where talks are short and yours is just one of many, your audience is not going to remember details. In such a situation, less is more. Give your auditors short, striking "punch lines" that they'll remember. They can always read your written work later, but if you don't get them interested and show them why it's important, they won't learn enough to *want* to read it.

Make an outline. Once you have your plan, reduce it to an outline. You can put this on paper (as notes for yourself), on slides (as bullet points), or in the notes section of your presentation software. (PowerPoint, for example, has a notes field that you can see but your audience cannot.) Your outline needs enough detail so that you can remember what to say, but no more. Ideally an outline consists of short phrases rather than complete sentences (which would tempt you to read them aloud). One strategy is to go through your paper and collect a series of sentence fragments; then rearrange these until you've got what you need. The outline view in word-processing software can be helpful for doing this.

Summarize at the beginning and again at the end. "Tell 'em what you're gonna tell 'em, tell 'em, and tell 'em what you told 'em." This classic principle still holds. Following this rule helps your audience get your main points. Even more important, it helps them *remember* what you said, which is, after all, why you're there. You can be creative about how you deliver such a summary. A few phrases can do the whole job, posing a puzzle or a problem you're about to solve and showing the way to the solution.

Talks need a sense of an ending. You'll develop your own style of ending a presentation. Make it completely clear when you are concluding. Show a slide headed "Conclusions." Or say, "To conclude . . ." or "To sum this up . . ." Even more important, though, you need a final sentence that really *sounds* like an ending, one that is spoken slowly and deliberately, with a falling intonation. *Practice delivering this before the talk.* After your final sentence, say something short and simple, such as "Thank you." Then stop talking and *wait* for applause. (If you're nervous, it can be tempting to try to fill the two seconds of silence that often occurs at this point. Don't.)

PRINCIPLES OF EFFECTIVE TALKS

No rule applies always and everywhere, but the following principles almost always make for better presentations.

Talk, rather than read. Written academic language is usually quite complex—far more complex than ordinary speech. So while good academic style can make beautiful reading, that doesn't translate into beautiful speaking. Sentences tend to be long, with many clauses and arcane vocabulary that becomes impossible to follow when read aloud.

Don't read. Just talk. You'll be easier to understand, and you'll make genuine contact with your audience. Furthermore, you'll think more clearly. If you can't communicate your points by talking (without reading), how well do you really understand what you want to say?

There are a few—very few—situations in which you may actually need to read aloud from a prepared text. If you are extremely nervous about presenting, if English is not your native language, or if you have a disability that makes extemporaneous speech difficult, the thing to do is to try to write a talk. To do this, make your plan and your outline, and then try to write out what you'll say in language that sounds natural when read aloud. *This will not be the same as the language of your paper.* Keep sentences short and simple. Avoid jargon and terms you would find difficult to explain if someone asked. If you are not a native speaker of English, avoid words or phrases you have trouble pronouncing.

If you really must do this, remember that 100 words per minute is about all you can hope for. Don't tell yourself you'll read really fast and cram in more words. You want to project a relaxed, confident presence, and you can't do that if you're desperately rushing to finish on time.

Stand up. If you can't see the faces of all your audience members, they can't see yours. So if people are sitting in rows, stand up, even if there are only a few people in the room. This lets people in the back rows see your face and hear you better. Standing also puts you in a dominant position. This sounds politically incorrect, but it's not. Remember, you're the focus. The audience *wants* you to be in charge, so go ahead and take the top-dog position, physically above their heads. The exception to this rule is in seminar-style presentations around a table with only a few people. In this situation, everyone can see you, and standing up usually seems too formal. At conferences, though, you should stand up even if other presenters on your panel have been sitting down.

Move around. It's easier to keep focused on someone who's moving than on a motionless talking head. Hand gestures are good, too. Don't hesitate to show your enthusiasm for your topic; it's infectious. It's possible to overdo this one, though. If you leap around like a rock star or stab the air with rap hands, you'll distract people from the content of your talk. Simply walking back and forth from one side of the room to the other every three to four minutes is usually enough.

Vary the pitch of your voice. Monotones are sleep inducing. Many people don't realize they do this. Get a trusted friend or colleague to listen to your delivery and give you honest feedback. (This is an important principle in itself!) Even better, tape or videotape yourself and check out how you sound and look. For more, see the section on vocal technique later in this chapter.

Make eye contact with your audience. If this is anxiety-inducing for you, at least *pretend* to make eye contact by casting your gaze toward the back and sides of the room. People will think you are looking at someone, even if you are only looking at the wall just above their heads. Another technique is to locate a few friendly individuals, at different places in the room, and speak directly to them, switching frequently from one to another.

Avoid "siding." Be careful not to ignore one side of the audience. Many speakers "side" unconsciously, looking always to the left or to the right half of the room, or only to the front or the back. Because it forces you to stand far to one side or the other, using a projector tends to amplify this effect. Moving back and forth periodically, from one side of the screen to the other, can minimize this effect.

Speakers also tend to concentrate on those who seem to be responding well (nodding, smiling, etc.). *This can be a trap.* In professional situations, it's often the people who are frowning, falling asleep, or seeming bored whom you most need to draw in. If looking at them directly makes you uneasy—and it *can* be extremely flustering—use the technique of casting your gaze just above their heads toward the back of the room.

Use visual aids. This is one of the most important principles of all. A good strategy for novice presenters is to project the outline of your talk. Some speakers seem to think they're giving everything away if they show people what they're going to say before they've said it. Instead, the effect of a good talk outline, well presented, is exactly the opposite: It makes your audience curious to hear the details. At the same time, it helps them follow the structure of your thinking. For more on this, see the section about presentation software later in this chapter.

Notice your audience and respond to needs. If people seem to be falling asleep or getting restless or distracted, the problem may not be you or your talk. Is the room too hot or too cold? Is it too dark or too noisy? Can people see you? Is the microphone on? Is something outside the room distracting people? Don't hesitate to stop talking in order to solve these problems. Alternatively, you may have gone on too long, or you may need to speak more loudly. Whatever the case, notice what's happening and use it as feedback. If you can't figure out why your audience is responding poorly, ask somebody later and fix the problem next time.

If you're not sure whether people can see or hear, *ask* someone in the back row directly. (This is also a good technique for setting up initial communication with your audience. It makes listeners feel included and puts you in touch with them as human beings.) Taking charge of the talk environment is part of your job as a speaker. *Never* let others control room conditions in ways not to your liking. For example, many "helpful" audience members react to the use of a projector by jumping up to turn off lights and close window shades. Unless this is truly necessary to see your images, avoid it at all costs, *especially* at conferences, which often take place in exceedingly dim hotel meeting rooms.

Practice everything, including improvising. The day before your talk, or even the morning before (or both), run through your entire talk at least once, preferably twice, *exactly as you plan to deliver it.* If your dry run doesn't sound right or doesn't fit into the allotted time, your actual performance won't either. So fix your talk, or cut it back, and then rehearse it again until you get it just right. Never tell yourself you'll fix it on the fly; this is bound to fail.

Until you've really mastered presenting, *never ever* try to improvise during a talk. This doesn't mean you can't interrupt yourself to tell a joke or a story, or digress a bit from the main thread—those can be important techniques for entertaining your audience, keeping their attention, and showing your human side. What it does mean is that *you must rehearse those things as well*, because they take time. If you haven't practiced them, you won't have any idea how long they take (usually a lot longer than you think). Like a professional comedian or actor, you need to practice *everything* you plan to do—including things you want your audience to think you're improvising.

Keep control of the stage. Sometimes people will interrupt you during your talk. If it's just a clarifying question and it's short, fine—answer it and move on. But much more time-consuming and flustering situations can occur.

I'm talking about the awkward situation in which somebody jumps in repeatedly, with long, loud comments or arguments in the middle of your talk. This can be extremely disturbing, especially for grad students at the bottom of the professional hierarchy. *Anticipate this* and plan a strategy for maintaining control. Unlike soccer games, talk periods don't get extended to make up for time-outs. You can't afford to spend 5 or 10 minutes on a digression in the middle of your presentation, because you won't get that time back.

The best techniques I've found are the following. First, you can cast a glance at whoever is chairing the conference session or your sponsor at a job talk. If you're lucky, that person will intervene on your behalf. Second, you can wait politely until the outburst stops and then say as calmly as possible something such as, "Thank you for your comment. I'd like to respond, but if you don't mind, I'll hold that for the question period."

Your last alternative takes nerves of steel, but sometimes there's no other choice. For example, your tormentor seems determined to drone on for ten minutes and nobody seems willing to stop him or her. This is when you need to say loudly but firmly, as authoritatively as you can, "Sir (or Madam), please allow me to finish my talk. I'll be happy to talk with you after the session." Pause for a long beat and then simply proceed and ignore further interruptions from that person. Remember, probably everyone in the audience is feeling your pain and is wishing for a way out of the situation. If you can muster the courage to shut the heckler down, others will pile on, and you'll be saved.

Test everything, including the room. Some rooms present speakers with uncomfortable or unusual situations, such as steeply raked seating that makes you feel like you're in a pit, or a podium that is 30 feet away from the first row of seats. Show up at the talk site at least 15 minutes early—30 minutes if possible—to check equipment, mount and test your slides, scope out the room, and get comfortable in the setting. Walk around, talk out loud, spend a little time imagining yourself giving the talk. Try to anticipate how it will feel and how you might need to adjust your performance to fit the situation.

Get 15 minutes of quiet time before the talk. To clear your mind and review your notes or slides, take 15 minutes before your talk in a different room (so that arriving audience members won't blow your concentration). At a conference, retreat to your hotel room or find an out-of-the-way lobby. At a job talk, a good host will plan for you to have at least 30 minutes alone immediately before you speak. If a break is not on your schedule, tell your host that you really need one and ask to have your schedule revised. Sometimes a host will hang around and keep talking to you while you're trying to gather yourself and review your notes. If this happens, ask politely but directly for a few minutes alone. During your quiet time, remember to breathe.

You're going to need well-oxygenated blood when you stand up to face the audience.

Emulate excellent speakers. The very best way to become an excellent speaker yourself is to watch really good, experienced speakers and model your talks on theirs. I'm sure your advisor is a great thinker or scientist. Unfortunately, this does not necessarily translate automatically into being a great performer. Academia is crawling with lousy speakers, so you may have to look hard to find a truly great role model. When you do find role models, notice not just what they say, but what they *do*: how they move, how they use their voices, how they look at the audience, how they handle timing and questions. (*Caution:* It's important to find someone in your field to emulate. Great political speaking styles, television-personality styles, and the like don't usually work well in academic settings. Respect the speaking conventions of your own social world.) If you find an excellent model and work hard to emulate that person, you can't go wrong. Your own style will come in time.

USING PRESENTATION SOFTWARE

People are visual creatures, and the old adage that a picture is worth a thousand words is especially true in presentations. Pictures, graphs, charts, cartoons, and other images can be extremely helpful. Keep them simple and uncluttered. Also, avoid dark images that won't show up well. Test *with an actual projector*; what looks great on your laptop may look pixilated or too dark on a projector screen.

Text slides, if you use them, should be extremely concise and visually uncluttered. Slides are maps, not territories; they are tracking devices that let both you and your audience follow the flow of the talk. Therefore, they must not be overfilled. Six lines of text per slide is plenty. Nine lines is a lot. Twelve lines is pretty much unreadable. Bullet points should be no more than a few words, and they should *not* be complete sentences.

If you need more text, use more slides. One of the beauties of presentation software is that you can have as many slides as you want. I've seen extremely effective presentations with only one word on most slides, only one image on many others.

Always choose white or light-colored slide backgrounds. Why? To see light text on dark slides, you'll have to turn down the lights, or even turn them off. This makes it hard to see your notes, the podium, and so forth. Worse, it will tend to put your audience to sleep. Really. By contrast, dark text on light-colored slides can usually be read with the lights on and the shades open.

Don't let your host, or anyone else, manage the lighting for you—say that you prefer to leave the lights on. If you can see it, your audience can probably see it too. If in doubt, walk to the back of the room and check. If you do have to turn the lights off to see a particularly dark slide, get somebody to turn them back on as soon as you're done.

Avoid overuse of video. In the context of a 15-minute talk, even one 3-minute video clip can seem interminable. More than one can make people want to scream. Videos also break the flow and eat up time better saved for your presentation. If you really need video for your topic, edit clips to an absolute minimum length. A good goal is 30 to 40 seconds.

Talk to the audience, not the screen. One of the worst presenter mistakes is to face the screen while talking. After all, everyone else is staring at the screen, so you may find yourself drawn to stare at it too. If you do this, the audience will be looking at your back, and they won't be able to hear you. Instead, have your laptop, or a paper version of your notes, in front of you. Speak from that, rather than from the slides on the screen. *This takes practice, practice, and more practice.*

Dial down the glitz factor. PowerPoint fades, transitions, backgrounds, sound effects, and so on can be real pitfalls. Glitzing up your presentations can turn into a serious time sink, detracting from the far more important time you spend on content. Also, these distractions can give your audience the impression that you care more about surface than substance. Finally, special effects can cause breakdowns during the presentation if they don't work as you expect them to. Nothing irritates an audience more than watching somebody fiddle frantically with a computer in the middle of a talk. So keep everything basic, at least until you've completely mastered the software. *Always practice the final version.*

Death by PowerPoint and what to do about it. One thing many novice presenters forget is that listening to someone read bullet points from a slide can be even more stupefying than listening to a paper being read. Your audience will usually read the entire slide in 15 seconds, far faster than you can read it aloud. So don't insult their intelligence by reciting it to them. Instead, use the bullet points mainly as memory jogs; speak about them and from them, without ever actually reading them aloud. Once again, the key is lots of practice beforehand.

In recent years, PowerPoint's bullet-list structure has been so overused that it can be more of a turnoff than a facilitator. If you are confident enough, a very effective technique is to speak only from images (and charts, figures, etc.), with minimal text and no bullet points. Printed notes, keyed to the slides, can guide you through what you want to say. Don't make yourself a slave to the software—use it creatively.

TIMING: AN ALL-IMPORTANT SKILL

Timing a talk well is among the most crucial of presentation skills. Nothing's more embarrassing, or more disastrous, than getting only halfway through your talk before hitting the time limit.

Finish within your time limit. Don't disrespect your audience by running overtime. *Never* go longer than the posted time limit. If you exceed this limit, you'll lose them at the crucial point, namely your conclusion. Whatever the time limit, respect it. Often, someone on the panel will be the timekeeper. This individual will have cards that denote the amount of time left and will show them to you at set intervals. Make sure you know where this person is sitting and glance over from time to time to stay on track.

In conference settings, exceeding your time limit is also incredibly rude, since it cuts into other speakers' allotted time or the discussion period. If an ineffective panel chair fails to restrain a speaker who runs over, wait a minute or so, then interrupt (politely) and say something like, "I'm sorry, but I'd like to be sure everyone on the panel has enough time for their talks." No one will hold that against you—others are certainly thinking the same thing, and your intervention will be greeted (by most people) with relief.

Use a timing device. You are (or are becoming) a professional presenter. So invest in a watch especially for this purpose. Some digital watches have countdown timers, which keep you from having to do mental math to know how much time remains. But these only work if (a) you remember to use the timer, (b) the numbers are large enough to read easily while you're talking, and (c) you're paying attention, so you can turn off the timer before it begins to beep.

PowerPoint's "Presenter View" has an embedded stopwatch. This is a great way to keep close track of your time. The problem, once again, is remembering to start the stopwatch at the beginning of your talk. (This turns out to be surprisingly hard.) I find it easiest to use an analog watch with large, easy-to-read hands.

Develop a standard slide. You can develop your sense of timing by always using the same format for text slides. After you've given a few talks with the same format, a little math will tell you how many minutes it usually takes you to talk through one slide. From there, you can estimate the length of a new talk from the number of slides.

Decide in advance what you can skip. Make a small mark on dispensable slides. Then, if you do run short on time or if your panel is running overtime, skip slides in the middle and jump to the conclusion so you can spend enough time on that. *Never* just plow ahead, talking faster and faster and trying to cram it all in. You'll only succeed in irritating your audience and forcing your host to cut you short. This can only end badly.

> **TIP:** Say you have 15 minutes to talk. When you're rehearsing, mark your notes or slides when you hit the 5-, 10-, and 13-minute points. That way you won't be caught by surprise if you start to run overtime.

Don't draw attention to timing problems. If you do run short on time, avoid saying anything about it. Talking about your own timing wastes words and makes your apparent lack of preparation the main focus. Instead, just pause, gather yourself, take a deep breath and a drink of water, and make some adjustments so you can finish on time: skip slides, say less about each one, and jump to the conclusion.

Practice, practice, practice. This point bears repeating. The only way to be sure you time things right is to rehearse your talk: every word of it, *exactly as you plan to deliver it.* Timing is a complicated, learned skill that requires a lot of practice, so practice where it's easy and comfortable—for example, at home or with other students.

SPEAKING FROM THE GUT: ABOUT VOCAL TECHNIQUE

Public speaking is much like singing. It takes a lot of air. You're going for volume, range, and effect. You want to fill the whole room with your voice; people in the back rows must be able to hear you clearly. Make a recording of yourself speaking in a large room. Do you talk in a monotone? Do you mumble? Do you speak too fast? Do you project confidence and authority, or does every statement come out sounding like a question?

Speak from the gut, not the throat. Learn about, and practice, diaphragmatic breathing (breathing from the belly, rather than the chest). Nervousness tends to make breathing shallow and rapid, but what you need is exactly the opposite. Breathe deeply. It's necessary to generate volume and will also help you keep your mind clear. If you don't breathe right, you can actually pass out from lack of oxygen. When you speak, push the air out with your diaphragm; and use plenty of air, just as a singer must do.

Speak at the bottom of your vocal range. Use your deepest pitch. This is also your loudest and most commanding tone, and it helps establish your legitimacy and authority. (This can be especially important for women.)

Most people don't realize how quietly they speak. If you're a quiet speaker, you may feel like you're shouting when you hit a volume adequate to fill a room. But it's better to be a bit too loud than too quiet. Aim your voice at the people in the last row, not those in the front. This takes considerable practice, especially to maintain a sufficient volume throughout a talk. If a microphone is available, it usually makes sense to use it.

Silence is a crucial element of speech. A continuous flow of sound soon becomes soporific. *Stop the flow periodically* by pausing briefly at the ends of sentences or between slides. Use these pauses to take a deep breath. Sometimes people drone on because they fear being interrupted. Remember, during a talk, people probably aren't going to interrupt you. You're in control anyway, so you don't have to accept interruptions if they do happen.

Use vocal "special effects." For example, echo key phrases. When you hit a phrase you want people to remember, "echo" it. Repeat it once; then move on. Also, pause for a few seconds—that's longer than you may realize—at several points in your talk. This gives you a chance to sip some water, which will lubricate your throat. These long pauses will often reawaken anyone who's tuned out.

HANDLING QUESTIONS

The Q&A period at the end of a talk can be one of the most difficult parts for inexperienced presenters. Here, as with everything else, spending some time anticipating likely questions and preparing your answers can reduce your anxiety and improve your performance. Practicing with a live audience and encouraging them to ask questions is the best way to do this. Here are a few other tips and strategies.

Get help from the audience. Sometimes you find a question incomprehensible, either because it is poorly expressed or because the speaker's English (or your own) isn't that great. In cases like these, don't hesitate to say, "I'm not sure I understand the question. Can someone help me?" This gives the audience permission to translate; usually someone will be able to reformulate the question in a more understandable way.

Hold something in reserve. Most talks are based on articles, book chapters, etc. Instead of trying to cram everything from the written piece into your talk—which is probably impossible anyway—hold back some of the interesting secondary points, data, or details. This strategy ensures that you'll still have something to say after the formal talk ends. Sometimes I will end the formal talk with a black slide but have several more slides waiting behind it for things I want to talk about that I couldn't fit in.

Divert difficult questions. Obviously, you should try to answer all questions on their own terms if you can. But what if you're stumped? I believe that if you don't know the answer to a question, you should say so. But if that's all you do, your response will be seen as a failure. To avoid this fate, you can say something like this: "That's a very interesting question. I'm not sure I have a good answer right now, but your question makes me remember that I wanted to say a few words about X . . ." Then fill in the X with one of the points you've held back—ideally, of course, one that connects somehow to the question. This may not work in a panel setting, but it is a good tip if you have to present as a sole speaker.

PLAN FOR DISASTER

Computers introduce many possible points of failure into presentations. So Murphy's Law—"whatever can go wrong, will go wrong"—applies, and *it applies directly to you.* Something can, and usually does, go wrong with the computer, the projector, the software, the connector cables, your thumb drive, or your presentation itself. Never assume that what works on a PC will work on a Mac or vice versa. You also can't assume your host will have the same version of PowerPoint (or Keynote, etc.) that you do. Inquire in advance.

Be prepared to use your own computer. I always prefer to project from my own machine, because I know its quirks and I know exactly how to connect it. You may prefer to use your host's, but bring your own and be prepared to use it, just in case.

Bring backup. My hard disk drive once crashed irretrievably on slide number three of a 45-minute talk. This kind of thing not only *can* happen to you, it *will* happen to you. The question isn't whether but when.

So, if you use a computer, *always bring backup.* Once again, that's *backup, backup, backup.* Because you're likely to be working on your talk until not long before you present it, begin making backups as soon as you start preparing the talk, and keep making them obsessively every hour or so until the talk is finished. Use a USB thumb drive or some other common medium. *Network backup is not reliable*, because you can't be sure you'll have an Internet connection. You can keep thumb drives in a pocket or hang them around your neck. That way, even if somebody steals your bag or your laptop, you've still got the backup. Two backups, stored in different places, is not an extreme idea.

Bring printed notes. If the projector commits suicide in the middle of your talk, you'll have no time at all to fix it. None. *Always be prepared to deliver your talk without any slides* as a last resort. This is where you will really be glad you brought printed notes. Speaking without slides is one thing, but speaking with no notes at all is a skill that only the greatest presenters ever master.

LAST WORDS

Practice everything. Test everything. Plan for disaster. Keep control of the situation. Breathe. Practice some more. But above all, be yourself—your audience is there to hear *you*.

FURTHER READING

Antropologi.info. "How to Present a Paper—or Can Anthropologists Talk?" Blog post, March 24, 2006. http://www.antropologi.info/blog/anthropology/2006/how_to_present_a_paper_or_can_anthropolo.

Colorado State University Writing Center. "Writing Guide: Informative Speaking." http://writing.colostate.edu/guides/speaking/infomod/index.cfm.

Monarth, Harrison, and Larina Kase. *The Confident Speaker: Beat Your Nerves and Communicate at Your Best*. New York: McGraw-Hill, 2007.

Purrington, Colin. "Gratuitous Advice on Giving a Talk." 2007. http://www.swarthmore.edu/NatSci/cpurrin1/powerpointadvice.htm.

Shewchuk, Jonathan. "Giving an Academic Talk." n.d. http://www.cs.berkeley.edu/~jrs/speaking.html.

Wakeford, Nina. "PowerPoint and the Crafting of Social Data." *Ethnographic Praxis in Industry Conference Proceedings* 2 (2006): 94–108.

RESOURCE

Presentations and slide examples
www.slideshare.net

4

Submitting and Getting an Article Accepted in a Journal

Tom Boellstorff

No matter how good your ideas may be and regardless of the quality of your research, your work will not have the influence it deserves unless you ensure it is published in appropriate journals. Publishing in journals is one of the most important considerations for hiring and promotion, including tenure. But publishing in journals is more than naked careerism or the pursuit of status: it is a crucial means for building a scholarly community and advancing intellectual inquiry. The peer-review and editorial process found at nearly all top journals works to improve the quality of our written work and helps it speak to the broadest audiences possible.

Despite all these advantages, the process of submitting a manuscript to a journal may seem intimidating. Some graduate programs offer a "professionalization" course, but even in the relatively rare cases in which such courses exist, discussion of submitting to a journal may be perfunctory. Yet despite the wide range of journals that publish anthropological research and the risk of rejection that attends the act of submitting a manuscript to a journal, it is clearly a worthwhile endeavor.

This chapter addresses scholars finishing their theses and dissertations, on the job market, or in tenure-track positions. However, it is pertinent to senior scholars as well. After tenure, the pressure to publish in journals decreases, and many senior scholars simply opt for less competitive venues. As editor in chief of *American Anthropologist*, I know that the review process can provide welcome feedback for more established scholars and can help disseminate their work to new audiences. In this chapter, I focus on what happens when

Reproduced by permission of the American Anthropological Association from *American Anthropologist* 113, no. 3 (2011).

you have written a manuscript that you think has a good chance of being accepted for publication at a top-notch journal. What do you do then?

SELECTING A VENUE

A wide range of journals publish anthropological research, and selecting a journal can seem daunting. I have several suggestions in this regard.

Journal Articles, Not Edited Volumes

First, "No chapters in edited volumes until tenure." This maxim may seem draconian, and there are worthwhile exceptions as I discuss here, but the draconian phrasing is easier to recall and drives the point home. For junior scholars, it can be flattering to be asked to contribute to an edited volume, particularly if the editor or editors are eminent figures to whom one might feel beholden (or at least at pains not to disappoint). In addition, some edited volumes gain wide circulation and are seen as benchmark publications in a field of scholarship.

Despite these temptations, in general it is best to decline invitations to have one's work published in edited volumes before tenure (with some caveats noted here). In obtaining tenure, but also more broadly in terms of establishing the quality of one's research, peer-reviewed journals are the gold standard, particularly when reviews are blinded, because they are managed by a general editorial process. Given that more and more scholars access publications online, it also bears noting that it is generally much easier to obtain journal articles via the Internet than chapters in edited volumes.

A key issue here is that while publishers will usually permit a few chapters in an edited volume to be previously published material, the inverse does not apply. With rare exceptions, manuscripts submitted to peer-reviewed journals must not have been previously published elsewhere. Sadly, there have been cases where scholars have published what they see as their best material in edited volumes without fully realizing that they have eliminated the possibility of publishing that material in a peer-reviewed journal. As a result, the ideal sequence is for a scholar to publish his or her work in a top peer-reviewed journal and then have that article reprinted in an edited volume.

As noted, there are some minor caveats to my tenet "No chapters in edited volumes until tenure." A single chapter in an edited volume, particularly if the editors are seen as key figures in one's research community, certainly does not detract from one's curriculum vitae. (However, if this means that a manuscript could have appeared in a top peer-reviewed journal, the decision may not have been the best trade-off.) What is of greater concern would be a tenure file that has three or four chapters in edited volumes but few or no articles in peer-reviewed journals. This can make it appear that a scholar is only able to publish work when relying on "insider" networks.

Another caveat concerns edited volumes for which the junior scholar in question is the editor or coeditor. Such an edited volume can help establish a junior scholar as a leader in his or her field, one who brings together colleagues in endeavors that advance intellectual conversations. However, managing the production of an edited volume is enormously time consuming. Thus, because there are only so many hours in the day, it bears emphasizing that the time involved in bringing an edited volume to fruition is time taken away from working on one's own research productivity. All things being equal, and barring some special set of circumstances, I recommend that junior scholars hold off editing an edited volume until after tenure.

The "Journal Triangle"

Returning to the primary topic of publishing in journals, the question, "Which journal should I pick?" looms large and can be a source of confusion to many junior scholars. There are now a number of resources that rank journals that publish anthropological research. It is beyond the scope of this chapter to engage in such rankings, but some key considerations for evaluating the reputation of various journals include the following:

- Citation calculations such as those done by Publish or Perish or ISI's impact factor
- Lists that rank journals by reputation
- Average time of review/time to publication (usually available on the journal's web page or by asking the editor)
- Acceptance rates or rejection rates (usually posted on the journal's web page).

I have included some resources in the "Further Reading" section.

Unfortunately, there are a few "predatory" publishers and journals with an uncertain scholarly reputation. It is critical to understand how your colleagues rate and evaluate journals so as to place your work in the most fitting journals possible.

An important consideration is that of coverage. For the review process leading to a hiring decision or tenure and also for ensuring one's general visibility as a scholar, it is crucial to demonstrate participation in a wide range of relevant scholarly communities.

As a convenient rule of thumb, I refer to the "journal triangle." My advice is that, as soon as possible (and ideally within three to five years after obtaining a tenure-track position), junior scholars publish research articles in "general," "area," and "topic" journals. Allow me to use my own scholarly history as an example. My dissertation focused on the lifeworlds of gay and lesbian Indonesians. Within five years of obtaining my Ph.D., I worked to publish research articles in general anthropological journals (including *American Anthropologist*, *American Ethnologist*, and *Cultural Anthropology*). Publishing in general journals shows that your work is legible and useful to a broad range of anthropological interests. I also worked to publish research articles in area studies journals (the *Journal of Asian Studies* and the *Asia Pacific Journal of Anthropology*). Publishing in area journals shows that your work participates in area-specific conversations in anthropology and beyond. Finally, I worked to publish research articles in journals focusing on questions of sexuality (*GLQ: A Journal of Gay and Lesbian Studies*). Publishing in topic journals shows that your work contributes to subjects of inquiry relevant to your research that cut across disciplinary and regional interests.

Hitting all three corners of the journal triangle in this manner is a far more effective way to build your career than publishing in only one type of journal (and certainly more effective than relying on edited volumes). Put yourself in the shoes of a person who has been asked to write a letter in support of your tenure. How much easier it is to write such a letter when the author can simply point out "this person's work is being published and cited in anthropology, in their regional scholarly community, and in venues concerned with the person's topic of study." Tenure letters where a writer waxes effusive about the quality of a scholar's work but can point to few examples demonstrating the actual impact of the scholarship in question are far less convincing than tenure letters in which writers can contextualize their praise by reminding a review committee of the broad palette of venues in which the scholar has published research.

Of course, I intend my notion of the journal triangle to be taken heuristically. For instance, I have conducted ethnographic research in the virtual world *Second Life*. For that scholarship, area and topic to some degree blur, as I publish in venues such as *Games and Culture* or *The Journal of Virtual World Research*. In addition, any research project addresses multiple topics (for instance, my Indonesia work is about globalization as much as it is about sexuality). However, the general goal remains valid: junior scholars should seek to publish in generalist anthropological journals, journals concerned in some sense with an area or region of study, and journals concerned in some sense with the topic of study. More broadly, all scholars (but particularly junior scholars) should seek to place their work in the widest range of top-notch journals possible because there is no better way to demonstrate that one is participating in a range of research communities.

UNDERSTANDING THE PEER-REVIEW PROCESS

Once you have decided where to submit your manuscript, and assuming you have selected a journal that uses peer review, you will become a participant in a key mechanism of scholarly publication, the peer-review process. Understanding how this process works can make the difference in whether your manuscript is accepted for publication. There are variations in how the peer-review process works for different journals but also sufficient commonalities so that it is possible to distill some general guidelines.

Preparing Your Manuscript for Submission

Once you have selected the first journal where you would like to submit your manuscript, the first thing to do is look carefully at that journal's guidelines or author instructions. At present, most journals have such guidelines on their web page. Even before initial submission, you may want to go back to your manuscript and make revisions based on an individual journal's guidelines, including questions of length and citation format.

In an ideal world, all journals would have identical guidelines for submission, but this is not the case. For instance, most journals limit the length of submissions. Sometimes this is still measured in pages, but increasingly the limit is measured in word count. Most journals want submissions in the range of 8,000 to 10,000 words. In most cases, that word limit is "all inclusive," meaning that everything is included in the word count—the main text as well as the bibliography, any footnotes or endnotes, any tables or appendixes, and so on. If you are using Microsoft Word, be sure you have the "include footnotes and endnotes" box checked when assessing your word count. Some journals will let slip a manuscript that goes a little over the word limit, but in a spirit of fairness, many journals simply unsubmit manuscripts that are over the word limit (or that violate any of their main submission guidelines) and ask authors to resubmit once they have met the journal's requirements for submission.

Most journals prefer that the manuscript be submitted as a single file (for instance, do not separate out your bibliography as a separate document). However, most journals do request that images, figures, and tables be uploaded as separate documents. Just make sure you are aware of their preferences.

Most top-ranked journals are "double blind"; this means not only that you do not know the names of the persons reviewing your manuscript but also that the reviewers do not know your name. In disciplines like anthropology, there is often a sense that double-blind peer review is a waste of time because reviewers can usually figure out who wrote a manuscript, but from my editorial experiences, in a surprising number of cases a reviewer will state confidently that "so-and-so is the author of this manuscript" and the reviewer will be wrong.

If you are submitting your manuscript to a journal that uses double-blind review, it is your responsibility to "anonymize" the manuscript before submission. Many journals will unsubmit and send back to you a manuscript that has not been correctly prepared in this manner. Anonymizing or "blinding" a manuscript involves more than just taking your name off of the title page. For instance, an anonymized manuscript should not include an "acknowledgments" section because this usually makes the author easy to identify; this can be added later should the manuscript be accepted for submission. If you cite yourself in the manuscript, you should replace a citation like "(Boellstorff 2006: 234)" with "(Author 2006: 234)," but then this citation should not appear in the bibliography at all. If you provide the title, publisher, and so on of a book or article you wrote, it would obviously be easy for any reviewer to ascertain your identity. Also be sure that your name does not appear in the document name. Were I to upload a manuscript to a journal named "Boellstorff_submission.doc," that would likely compromise double-blinded peer review, and I might be asked to rename and resubmit the manuscript at the outset.

Submitting the Manuscript

Once you have prepared your manuscript for a particular journal, it is time to take the plunge and go through the submission process. A few journals still only accept paper submissions sent through regular mail, and a few require hard copies and online submission, but the vast majority of journals now accept submissions exclusively online. In a few cases, online submission simply means e-mailing your manuscript to the editor or to a support staff member at the journal, but online submissions now usually involve some kind of web-based submission system. Deal with it. Nothing is more annoying to editors and their support staff than authors who require hand-holding through the submission process. If you have the smarts to obtain a Ph.D. and conduct anthropological research, you can navigate an online submission system.

Most online submission systems require you to first register with basic information about yourself, including a workplace address and e-mail. In addition to actually uploading the manuscript, there will often be a series of questions for the author or authors. This often includes things like keywords as well as confirmation that the manuscript meets the journal's guidelines, is based on research for which proper human subjects clearance was obtained, and is not under consideration elsewhere (you should never submit a manuscript to more than one journal at a time). There is usually a place for authors to upload or type in a cover letter. At this stage, a cover letter is a good thing to do (it will reinforce your professionalism), but it should be very brief, simply stating that you are submitting the manuscript and are happy to answer any questions.

Online systems also typically provide authors with a place to list preferred and nonpreferred reviewers. It is wise to provide journals with a list of two to four preferred reviewers. Most editors (including myself) would never employ only preferred reviewers but have nothing against one of three or four reviewers being a preferred reviewer. Naming preferred reviewers saves journals time in terms of identifying scholars appropriate for reviewing your manuscript. Sometimes a preferred reviewer can be a sympathetic reviewer—a colleague or even a friend—but surprisingly often this "preferred" reviewer has the most negative assessment of the manuscript.

My advice is to be much more wary of listing nonpreferred reviewers (that is, persons you do not want to review your work) when submitting a manuscript—or in any other context. (Indeed, I take it as a point of pride that for my promotion to professor, I did not list a single nonpreferred scholar.) Unfortunately, there are cases where, due to personal rivalry, collegial misunderstanding, or turf wars between different perspectives or theoretical approaches in a field of inquiry, an author believes that certain individuals would not provide a fair assessment of the manuscript. If this is truly necessary, I advise listing the smallest number of nonpreferred reviewers possible. A long list of nonpreferred reviewers can be seen as a red flag that the author is combative or simply lacks standing in the scholarly community.

The Art of Waiting

Once you have submitted your manuscript, you have no choice but to wait for a reply. Most editors do an initial screening of manuscripts. Should that be the case and should the editor decide that your manuscript is not appropriate to send out for full review, you will probably receive a rejection letter within a week to a month.

Should the manuscript go out for full review, the editor will have to find some number of reviewers to assess your manuscript (usually from three to five, but sometimes as few as one or two, and sometimes as many as eight or more). Typically, about double to triple the number of desired reviewers must be asked before a sufficient number agree. Then the reviewers are provided some length of time (usually three weeks to three months) to prepare and submit their comments. Some reviewers can be months late in returning their reviews, at times forcing an editor to seek additional reviewers. Once all the reviews are in, the editor must read your manuscript and the reviews, make a decision, and then respond to you, often by writing an editor's letter of some kind.

This process takes time. The swiftest these various steps can take place is about one month, but far more common is three to four months, and sometimes six months or more. Particularly for junior scholars, this waiting period can be unnerving, which is yet another reason why it is so important to try to get manuscripts submitted to peer-reviewed journals within the first three years post-Ph.D. As editor in chief of *American Anthropologist*, I have occasionally been contacted by authors with a missive on some variation of "I am going up for tenure this year. Is there any way you can get a decision to me quickly?" Unfortunately, there is rarely anything I (or any editor) can do to force things along more rapidly, and in any case such a missive may indicate that the authors in question have failed to get their work into review sufficiently early in their career.

Even when questions of promotion are not pressing, you may feel you have been waiting an inordinately long time to hear back from a journal. If you wish to contact the journal, my first suggestion is that you do your homework and use the journal's web page to determine the administrative contact for the journal. Often this person will have a title like "editorial assistant." If no name is listed, the key thing to look for is the e-mail address for the journal—not the e-mail address of the editor! Only as a last resort should you ever contact the editor directly. Some authors inexplicably think "going to the top" and sending an e-mail to the personal e-mail address of the editor will result in the swiftest response. This is inadvisable for several reasons, including the fact that it is usually administrative staff who handle the online submission system on a daily basis and are best positioned to check on a manuscript. Another reason attempting to contact the editor directly is inadvisable is that many editors struggle to segregate their research and teaching work from their editorial duties by avoiding use of their personal e-mail accounts for editorial work.

Usually journal staff (including the editor) will not be able to give you a specific reason for a delay in obtaining a decision regarding your manuscript. The most common reasons for such delays are probably a reviewer failing to return the comments or a backlog of manuscripts in the editor's own "to-do" queue. However, in some cases an author query can motivate journal staff to hound tardy reviewers again or even to seek another reviewer. Overall, then, my advice to authors waiting for decisions is "Be patient and work on something else," but also that, after six months or so, a discreet, polite query to a journal's staff—remember, not to the editor directly—is acceptable.

Dealing with the First Rejection Letter

On a handful of occasions, I have been happy to provide an author with an "accept" decision after a first round of reviews. However, this has been extremely rare. Like most top-ranked peer-reviewed journals, *American Anthropologist* has an informal in-house rule along the lines of "We never accept manuscripts on the first round." In other words, almost all manuscripts published in top-ranked peer-reviewed journals first received a "revise and resubmit" decision. To avoid misunderstanding, most editors are careful to phrase revise and resubmit letters so as to make it formally clear that the manuscript has been rejected. It is emphatically not the case that if you do everything the editor asks of you in the revise and resubmit letter your manuscript will definitely be published. However, responding to the first rejection letter appropriately can greatly increase the chances of your article eventually being accepted for publication.

First, take heart and do not take criticism personally. Particularly for junior scholars having recently completed their graduate training in a department that (ideally) provided largely positive feedback, the experience of negative criticism can be jarring. Most editors work hard to cast their comments in the most constructive and supportive manner possible, and many also redact reviewer comments in cases where a reviewer makes overly dismissive or ad hominem comments (which in my experience is rare). Nonetheless, comments regarding the shortcomings of your work can be difficult to take. One way to reframe criticism is to think, "How is it that the reviewers have misunderstood my argument, and how can I modify my manuscript so as to minimize to the greatest degree possible the chance that other readers will make this misinterpretation?"

Second, do not resist. Do everything the editor and reviewers recommend. Many editors will synthesize reviewer comments in a separate editor's letter that includes specific recommendations for revision. Other editors simply forward reviewer comments with at most a short paragraph of synthetic comments. In any case, you should revise your manuscript in such a way as to take these comments into account. You may not like some of the suggestions. For instance, you may think that your review of relevant literatures is sufficient, while the editor may ask for that aspect of the manuscript to be expanded. In this case, what you like should take a backseat to the editor's recommendations. There are two reasons for this. First, if you do everything the editor suggests, it makes it more likely (though still not guaranteed) that your revised manuscript will be accepted for publication. Second, in retrospect it is usually clear that the editor and reviewers in question have identified legitimate weaknesses in your draft, ones that readers themselves would find compromise the manuscript's effectiveness.

Thus, the best thing to do is sit down with the reviewers' comments and the editor's comments (if any) and draw up a plan for how you will revise the manuscript so as to take these comments into account. It will occasionally happen that reviewers disagree: one will say, "You need more historical background," while another will say, "You need to trim down the historical background." In such cases, it is your responsibility to find a way to navigate the conflicting recommendations. In this example, for instance, the answer might be, "I need a more effective historical background" or "I need to cite more work, thus demonstrating background knowledge, but be judicious in my description of the historical context." Some editors provide authors with an expanded word limit for their revised manuscript. Under my editorship, for instance, *American Anthropologist* typically raises the word limit for revised and resubmitted manuscripts from 8,000 to 9,500 words. Even in such a case, some trimming down of the existing argument may be necessary to incorporate the needed revisions. Other editors provide authors with no additional word limit at all; in such circumstances, the author must simply find ways to edit down the existing manuscript so there is space for needed revisions.

I noted earlier that the cover letter accompanying an initial submission can be quite succinct. In contrast, the cover letter accompanying a revised and resubmitted manuscript should be more extensive. In addition to thanking the editor and reviewers, it should provide a road map reminding the editor of the main points for revision and demonstrating how the author has revised the manuscript to address these concerns (with page numbers identifying where in the revised manuscript the various improvements can be found). This makes it much easier for the editor to begin the review process for the revised manuscript.

Editors are occasionally able to render a decision of accept or reject (or even another revise and resubmit) based on their own reading of the revised manuscript. In most cases, however, editors put the revised manuscript through another full review process before making a decision. When this happens, editors often attempt to obtain at least three reviews, including at least one from an original reviewer and at least one from a new reviewer. Because this process obviously takes time, it is in your interest to have the shortest possible turnaround between receiving a revise-and-resubmit decision and resubmitting a revised version of the manuscript in question. If you can send in your revised manuscript within two to three months, you will receive a decision that much more swiftly. Even if your manuscript is eventually rejected, your efforts will not have been in vain, as you will be left with a substantially improved manuscript which you can submit to a different journal.

CONCLUSION

I hope these suggestions will help head off uncertainty and confusion regarding the world of journal publishing. Submitting manuscripts to journals can be scary, but it is a crucial way to support your career and also to move scholarly conversations forward. There are, of course, many other venues and modalities for intellectual work in anthropology and beyond, but journals play a vital role. Understanding how to submit your work to a journal will help you prepare more effectively, increase your chances of success, and make the entire process more useful—not just for your career but also for your own intellectual growth.

FURTHER READING

Beall, Jeffrey. "'Predatory' Open-Access Scholarly Publishers." *Charleston Advisor*, April 2010: 10.

Boellstorff, Tom. "How to Get an Article Accepted at *American Anthropologist* (or Anywhere)." *American Anthropologist* 110, no. 3 (2008): 281–283.

Boellstorff, Tom. "Acceptance and Rejection." *American Anthropologist* 110, no. 4 (2008): 409–411.

Boellstorff, Tom. "How to Get an Article Accepted at *American Anthropologist* (or Anywhere), Part 2." *American Anthropologist* 112, no. 3 (2010): 353–356.

RESOURCES

One type of software that tracks citations is Publish or Perish
http://www.harzing.com/pop.htm

One example of a list of journals and their rankings in Anthropology
http://www.aaanet.org/publications/list-of-journals.cfm

5

Publishing Your Dissertation as a Monograph

Sarah Caro

The reasons for wishing to publish your dissertation as a monograph are fairly obvious. You will have invested several years of your life and a lot of hard work into producing it, so why settle for simply securing your doctorate when you could be helping yourself on to the next stage of the career ladder by publishing a book as well? In some subfields of anthropology, the book-length publication can be an important addition to your C.V. Unfortunately, publishing your dissertation is unlikely to be that simple. Revising your thesis into a decent book involves a huge amount of work and could well prove as time consuming as writing a completely new book from scratch.

For some works, it is also debatable just how valuable an addition to the scholarly record it will really be. However hard you work to transform the material into book form, you will never be able to entirely hide the fact that it is a revised and extended Ph.D. thesis. There is also the question of whether the market can sustain another book in your specialist area. What makes a good topic for a Ph.D. thesis does not necessarily make a good topic for a book. Generally, good books (as opposed to good theses) will engage with broader scholastic themes and debates and appeal to a wider audience, both within and outside of anthropology.

> **TIP:** Go into your local library or campus bookshop (or type a few keywords into Amazon), and having identified the five or ten books that are the closest matches to your dissertation, try to make a list of what your proposed book would offer that none of the other books could provide.

If you still think your book would have something original to offer, talk to your supervisor, other senior members of staff, friends, and colleagues and ask them which key areas of research your work could tap into. If they all encourage you, the rest of this chapter will provide you with some basic guidelines on how to go about getting it published.

REVISING YOUR DISSERTATION

So why is it so hard to transform your Ph.D. thesis into a publishable monograph? The answer lies in their very different functions. Put crudely, the point of a thesis is to show its very small audience of experts that the author knows the literature, has mastered the necessary theoretical and methodological skills, and has something moderately interesting to say on a fairly narrow topic. Thus a doctoral thesis will include separate chapters on methodology, literature, and a very detailed bibliography. A monograph, in contrast, is written for a broader academic audience and will cover a range of results and topics. It is unlikely to have separate chapters devoted to methodology or literature, but rather discussions of both will be integrated into the narrative framework of the book as and when appropriate.

Restructuring

Bearing this in mind, you will need to ditch the structure of your thesis (without ditching all of the material!) and find a new, more integrated narrative through which to tell your story, focusing on those elements of your thesis that are genuinely original, be they theoretical or empirical or both. Each chapter will need to synthesize theory, data, and literature and build upon the previous chapter so that there is a clear progression and development of the argument. Often chapters on methodology, exhaustive background surveys demonstrating your familiarity with the giants in the field before you, and long exegeses on theory are no longer necessary for the monograph.

In the course of rethinking your original dissertation material, you may well find that there is not quite enough to sustain a 60,000-word book, especially as you will be trying to appeal to a broader audience. This is a common experience and can be addressed in a number of ways, including the following:

- adopting a comparative approach across countries or times
- applying a variety of methodological approaches to analyzing your data
- including secondary as well as original data

- using a range of theoretical perspectives
- adopting a cross-disciplinary approach
- exploring a particular theme across a whole body of work rather than just one particular theorist/country/field study.

All of the these will involve considerable extra work and may delay publication, so run your ideas for revision by colleagues and advisors and even consider putting together a proposal outlining the planned changes that you could send out to a few publishers to test the waters. If you get a positive response, you are obviously on the right track and it is worth investing the time and effort necessary to make the revisions. If not, you will have to seriously reconsider whether a book is the best option for you, and if you remain convinced that it is, you will need to explore new ways to expand and develop your material.

Style

As well as thinking about structure, you will also need to be aware of the style of writing appropriate to a monograph. One of the most frequent criticisms of Ph.D. theses is that they are overly reliant on the opinions of others—in other words they contain too many direct quotations from other critics and scholars. While it is important to position your work in relation to that of others and to show how your ideas build on and develop what has gone before, excessive block quotations can distract from and weaken your argument. Wherever possible, paraphrase or summarize rather than reproducing an argument verbatim, while making sure that you scrupulously reference any ideas that aren't your own.

More generally, keep it simple. Good academic writing should be clear and concise, and it should only include technical terminology where an ordinary word will not do because it lacks the necessary precision or nuance.

FINDING A PUBLISHER

Academic publishers are essentially conservative creatures. They are generally not interested in innovation or breaking into new fields. Therefore, the first thing you should do when thinking about which publishers to approach is look at your own bookshelves and repeat the exercise you did to determine whether there might be a market for your book. Look in the bookshop, look online, and chances are you will find that there is a relatively small number of publishers active in your particular area.

> **TIP:** Look at the imprints and publishers of the books you find in your area and identify series so that you can target your proposal more accurately in due course.

Next, talk to your colleagues, especially the more senior ones who have already published, and ask them about their perceptions of different publishers and their experiences of working with different editors. There is wide variation in working practices, expectations, and company cultures, and it can be useful to have some sense of this when choosing your publisher. The people you talk to may also have some personal contacts, or at least names, that they are prepared to share with you, the benefits of which are obvious. A recommendation from an established academic that the editor may know by reputation, if not personally, immediately enables the editor to place your work in some kind of context and will certainly increase the chances of your proposal being considered seriously. Be careful how you use such recommendations. They are very valuable, but they should be used in conjunction with a proper proposal and covering letter, not as a substitute for them.

Another very good way to get a sense of which publishers are currently active in your area is to visit the publisher exhibitions at conferences you attend. Exhibiting at these conferences is costly, so publishers go only to those conferences devoted to areas in which they already have a strong presence or are hoping to move into. Half an hour browsing the various stands, picking up catalogues, and taking flyers, will give you a good sense of which titles are being actively promoted and will give you the opportunity to ask whoever is at the stand about key titles for the coming season and which areas they are actively developing. Don't ask them if they will publish your book, but do ask them to whom proposals should be sent.

Of course all publishers now have their own websites where you can access information about their current program, backlist, organizational structure, and instructions on submitting a proposal (more on which in the next section). Spending some time browsing the websites of the key publishing companies in your area will provide you with essential information about their current commissioning program and will give you an opportunity to think about how your book might fit into it.

Finally, the question everyone asks is, "Are some publishers more prestigious than others?" There are certainly no league tables for publishers, and because they have to constantly adapt to a rapidly changing market, reputations can fluctuate. Yet, if you talk to established scholars in your field, you will soon find that some publishers are much more respected than others, usually due to the fact that they employ a full and rigorous review and development process resulting in a consistently high quality of publications. Members of the Association of American University Presses agree to certify their books through peer review, which is why in the United States these presses carry a great deal of prestige.

PREPARING AND PRESENTING A PROPOSAL

Having identified a list of potential publishers and thought about how to revise your dissertation, the next stage is to put together a proposal and cover letter to send out. The perfect proposal persuades the reader of the fascinating and original nature of its subject matter, the clarity and elegance of its style, and, above all, the quality of its scholarship. Anything that enhances and reinforces these properties is to be encouraged. Anything that detracts from them should be shunned.

> **TIP:** You will need to think about a new title for your book to distinguish it from your thesis. Choose a title that has as wide an appeal as possible and makes it easy to identify the general area. A short main title such as *Women, Health, and Ethnicity* works well with a more descriptive subtitle such as *A Study of Three Generations of African Americans Living in the Projects.*

Look at the website of your favored publisher. The vast majority of publishers' websites now include detailed guidelines for first-time authors on submitting a proposal, and though there is some variation as to how much sample material they like you to submit with the proposal, there is a clear consensus that good proposals should include the following:

Rationale/Overview/Statement of Aims

Whatever you choose to call this section of the proposal, it is the most important part of the whole thing and where you will generally win or lose your prospective editor. Take time, and work through several drafts. Don't assume a tone that is overly familiar and casual, but equally avoid sounding pompous and overblown. You need to clearly state the aims and objectives of the book; tell the reader what it's about, what approach you have taken and why, and your reasons for wanting to write this book now. This section should enable the editor to immediately contextualize your proposal so that he or she can tell at a glance what the proposed book's subject matter is and how it might fit into the list and the existing literature. Like a good book blurb, it has to draw the editor in and make the editor want to learn more.

Table of Contents

This should include a list of chapter titles and a paragraph or two on each chapter covering the key ideas and themes. You do not want to get bogged down with too much detail in producing these summaries but rather concentrate on conveying the scope of the material you intend to cover and emphasizing what is original or different about your treatment of the material.

> **TIP:** If you remember to include a preface and acknowledgments at the beginning and bibliography/references and index at the end of the proposed contents page, your proposal will look more professional.

Reader/Market

Defining the reader and market is actually much trickier than it sounds. If you claim that the book will appeal to everyone, the editor will think you don't know what you're talking about. If you are too cautious, however, and suggest that the book might only be of interest to a handful of scholars, you will remove any incentive for the editor to take a risk on your book. Instead, you should identify the core market for the book and any feasible additional or supplementary markets, clearly distinguishing between them. If there is a specific geographic market, Asian or Latin American, for instance, you should make that clear, as well as the level at which it is pitched. In other words, is it only suitable for postgraduates and scholars, or would it be accessible to advanced undergraduates?

Competition

Even if you are genuinely convinced that your book is unique, to put "None" under the heading "Competition" looks like you simply aren't trying, or, even worse, that you are not familiar with the literature. It is quite possible there are no other books *exactly* like yours, but paradoxically this is not necessarily a good thing. It may be that it is generally considered too narrow an area/perspective/approach to justify and sustain a book-length treatment. Hopefully you will have already thought carefully about the real gap in the literature you will fill, and also what other titles are similar. List those books that come closest to yours in terms of scope and approach and explain how yours differs from them.

Practical Details

Finally, it is worth having a short section at the end of the proposal that indicates your expected delivery date, the proposed length in pages or thousands of words, and the number of figures and tables and any illustrated material you are hoping to use, including photographs and maps. Try to make this as accurate as possible, but bear in mind that the more illustrations you use and the greater the length, the more expensive the book will be to produce. This will inevitably impact the editor's decision as to whether to pursue the project further, both from a point of view of cost and potential hassle. One way around this is to suggest putting material that is expensive to reproduce or likely to date on a dedicated website that you would maintain but that could be linked directly to the publisher's web page. You will obviously need to have a web page of your own that you can use in this way or the necessary skills to set one up (or someone willing to help you), but you do not need to go into very much detail at this stage.

THE PERFECT COVER LETTER

The perfect cover letter should be short, clear, and to the point. Whether it is an e-mail message or an actual piece of paper, it is vital to your chances of success that the editor reading it can tell at a glance (a) what you are asking (to consider your proposal for review), (b) what your project is about (is it a subject of interest?), and (c) who you are (is this a serious proposition?).

Although it may seem like an obvious point, take the time to find out the relevant editor's name (this will usually be listed on the publisher's website), and use plain paper if you are submitting hard copy, and black type and a clear font such as Times New Roman or Arial for hard or electronic copy, as they are easy to read and won't distract from the content. Make sure your full contact details and affiliation are easily identifiable. Finally, close your letter by making it clear that you have not chosen to approach this particular publisher at random, but because you admire and are familiar with their list and think your book would complement their current publishing program.

Following Up

Once you have sent your cover letter and proposal off, you will have to wait patiently, either for a simple acknowledgment of receipt or to hear whether the project will be sent out for review. Editors do not take kindly to being chased and may respond under pressure with a swift decline. If, however, after a month or so you have not received an acknowledgment of receipt, I think it is acceptable to follow up, but some editors may not agree. You alone will have to decide whether you think it is a risk worth taking or whether you are prepared to wait possibly several months for a reply.

TIP: If you do decide to follow up either by e-mail or telephone, try to find out whether the editor has an assistant and then contact the assistant. Always say you are simply checking on whether your proposal has been received and ask whether there is any further information you can provide.

I am often asked whether a potential author should approach a list of possible publishers one at a time, or should they be approached simultaneously? My instinct as a publisher is to say one at a time, but I suspect the truth is that it is fine to approach several at the same time as long as you make it clear to the publishers that this is what you are doing and don't try to play them off against each other—a strategy that could easily backfire.

SURVIVING THE REVIEWS

For author and editor alike, the most burdensome and frustrating part of getting an academic book published is the review process. Finding suitable reviewers for a proposal can involve considerable time and effort for even the most experienced editor, while for a first-time author, waiting for reviews is an agonizing experience. However, peer review is also potentially the most important and rewarding stage of the publishing process, as it enables the editor to make an informed assessment of a potential addition to the list and provides the author with very valuable feedback on the strengths and weaknesses of the proposal.

Peer review is the standard review process adopted by book and journal editors for assessing potential publications and involves your proposal or article being sent out to a number of anonymous reviewers (usually at least two, occasionally more). Reviewers are chosen for their expertise, but by remaining anonymous they are free to provide a completely honest report without fear of recrimination. Reviewers are usually asked to address a number of questions in their report such as the potential contribution to the field, the appropriate organization and presentation of the material, and the expected audience.

When you finally receive the reviewers' reports, whatever your initial feelings, do and say nothing except to acknowledge receipt and indicate when you will be able to send the editor your formal response. It is absolutely crucial that, however good or bad the reviewers' comments are, you give yourself time to overcome your initial feelings of anger, frustration, confusion, or relief and put together a detailed and considered response. Read through the reviews several times and discuss them with friends and colleagues whom you can trust not just to be supportive but to help you understand exactly what the reviewer is saying. When you are putting your formal response together, you should bear the following points in mind:

- Writing reviews is not an exact science, so there may well be contradictions and ambiguities that you need the help of others to unravel.
- Often a review that seems at first glance unremittingly negative, when broken down and responded to point by point, is not so bad!
- Always try to start with something positive. Thank the editor for the reviews and the opportunity to respond to them. This shows an awareness of the process and a willingness to consider feedback.
- Next, go through the reviews picking out all of the positive points. Dwell on them just long enough to make the point.
- Deal with any queries about possible content so that if a reviewer asks whether a topic is going to be covered and it is, say so and explain where and how. If not, don't be afraid to say you will not be covering it because it is not directly relevant.
- Address the not-so-positive points one by one. Missing literature references are easily supplied, and structures can be revised. One common but no less frustrating criticism is that in the reviewer's opinion the work is competent but says nothing new. In that case you should clearly and patiently reiterate what your original contribution will be, whether it takes the form of a new theoretical argument, new data, or new research on a new topic.

Finally, all that remains to be said is good luck! If you follow the guidelines laid out in this chapter, you are not guaranteed to get your thesis published, but your chances of doing so will have considerably increased.

FURTHER READING

Caro, Sarah. *How to Publish Your PhD: A Practical Guide for the Humanities and Social Sciences*. London: Sage Publications, 2009.

Germano, William. *From Dissertation to Book*. Chicago: University of Chicago Press, 2005.

RESOURCE

The Association of American University Presses publishes a very handy directory each year to North American university presses, providing details about topical areas of acquisition and the editors at those presses:

http://www.aaupnet.org/resources/publications.html#directory

Part II

SUBDISCIPLINARY CONSIDERATIONS

6

Archaeology

William Green and Linda Forman

It's easy to publish in archaeology, right? Just spend a few weeks on a site or a survey, analyze the artifacts, make a few maps, write up the project, and send off the report. Sounds pretty simple. And often it is. Practically every state and province in North America has an archaeology journal whose editor would love to receive a decent submission. The abundance of outlets affords great opportunities for publishing in archaeology. Moreover, the "gray literature" of limited-distribution cultural resource management (CRM) reports includes many gems that deserve publication. This chapter provides guidance about publishing your work in ways that are most useful to you and your intended audience.

In the words of Kent Flannery's "Old Timer," "Archeology is the only branch of anthropology where we kill our informants in the process of studying them" (1982: 275). The sites and features you excavate, the contexts you disturb, will continue to "exist" only in memory, in physical and virtual repositories and in the published record. This means, among other things, that, if you do archaeology, you also take on the responsibility of writing as clearly as possible and publishing in appropriate, accessible outlets. In addition to this ethical duty, publishing is a critical responsibility for archaeologists with career considerations such as getting an academic job, promotion, and tenure. This chapter is intended to help you identify appropriate venues for your work and to make the manuscript preparation and submittal process as productive as possible. (For a comprehensive review of the issues involved in communicating archaeological research, see Zimmerman 2003; for a survey of how academic archaeologists assess and select publication media and outlets, see Harley et al. 2010.)

CONFERENCES AND MULTIMEDIA

As noted in part I, conferences provide important opportunities to prepare, present, and discuss papers you can develop into publications. Whether you organize a session yourself, are invited to participate in an organized symposium, or volunteer your paper for an open session, you and your ideas will benefit from the exposure among peers and the feedback that can result.

Numerous opportunities exist to present and discuss archaeological work. Annual conferences of national, regional, state, and specialized societies all provide useful venues. You may not need to search any farther than your own backyard. Your local archaeological society is probably looking for speakers for its monthly meetings. Try your paper out at several conferences if you can, recognizing that you may need to rework, say, an Iowa Archeological Society presentation to make it appropriate for the Society for American Archaeology (SAA). But note also that even though the SAA presentation may look better to your dean or department chair, state and regional meetings often generate valuable feedback and suggestions for improving your manuscript. Don't dismiss an opportunity to present and polish your work simply because the venue may not appear prestigious.

Organized symposia often develop into edited volumes. Writing chapters for such books can be rewarding but frustrating too if even one contributor does not meet deadlines and the publication schedule lags. Book chapters may make your work visible and surround it with work on related subjects. However, while most publishers subject edited volumes to peer review, book chapters don't carry the same weight in promotion and tenure decisions as articles in prestigious journals. By all means, do *not* take on the task of editing a book yourself until you have participated as a contributor to at least one such volume and are able to devote an enormous amount of time to the project.

Electronic outlets such as websites, blogs, interactive videos, virtual exhibits, and podcasts are gaining importance in archaeology and are great ways to share research widely and creatively. Graduate students and CRM practitioners have prepared some remarkable electronic resources in archaeology. Unfortunately, new media venues have outpaced traditional academic reward systems, so it is difficult to recommend that tenure-track archaeologists devote substantial effort to such innovative and important work. Wait until you have tenure to roll out your big new-media projects.

THE BIG DECISION

Once you have a manuscript that has been battle tested in one or more conferences, you will need to decide whether you want your piece peer reviewed.

This decision may seem like a no-brainer. As noted in part I, peer review of manuscripts helps maintain and improve the quality of published work. Peer-reviewed publications form the linchpin of professional discourse and advancement, so, of course, you should seek to publish in such venues. But many archaeological publication outlets are not peer reviewed. Should you avoid them? Not necessarily. Nonreviewed journals provide opportunities for you to practice writing publishable manuscripts and to obtain rapid visibility in a particular state or region, and this exposure may be critical in the CRM field. The downside of publishing in these journals, in addition to not helping you get promoted or tenured, is that you might write something really awful. Publishing a bad article may harm you more than not publishing at all. So ask people you trust to read your manuscript before submitting it. And weigh the value of the time you spend preparing that manuscript against the time you could be spending on one for a peer-reviewed journal. Or, if you've located a nonreviewed outlet that is otherwise well suited to your needs, ask the editor to subject your manuscript to peer review and be sure the editor notes this when it is published.

Be an Anthropologist

Every publisher and journal has its own culture. Once you've chosen a set of relevant journals or publishers, do a bit of ethnographic research: be an anthropologist and learn about their cultures. Read recent and past issues of the journals. Do you detect trends in the kinds of articles published? Consult with people associated with the journals—the editor(s), editorial board members, published authors, and readers. How does the review process work? What are the rates of acceptance, rejection, and return for revision? How long does the review process take? Ask about the journals' impact factor ratings and professional reputations.

After you complete your mini-ethnography, look again at your manuscript. If you have a polished piece that needs an outlet, find a compatible publisher or journal. You may want rapid review and publication, or high-profile international exposure, or a specialized regional or topical audience. Don't waste time with an outlet whose turn-around time, theoretical orientation, or reputation doesn't meet your interests or needs.

Journals

A journal exists for practically every imaginable subject in archaeology. Take some time to scan the publishing landscape when considering appropriate outlets for your work. Don't send every paper to *American Antiquity*, but, by the same token, don't assume that a specialized or regional journal is the only venue for research you think is of limited interest. High-profile journals often publish local case studies and methodologically innovative work if reviewers and editors see broader implications or cutting-edge approaches.

Table 6.1 lists examples of different kinds of English-language archaeological journals of international, national, or regional impact. Nearly all use peer review. You can locate scores of other journals online or through state and provincial professional and avocational archaeological associations. Get to know journals of interest by looking at sample issues (publishers often provide online access), browsing recent issues in libraries, or subscribing.

Books

If you are trying to publish your dissertation, CRM report, or other lengthy manuscript as a monograph, your research into possible publishers will probably turn up several "usual suspects": university presses, commercial presses with solid archaeology lists, and specialty presses associated with research institutes, archaeological associations, and other nonprofits. A plethora of outlets exists for monographic publications. Added bonus: At some presses, archaeologists are even directors or acquisition editors! After your ethnographic work among colleagues turns up these names, contact these archaeologist-publishers directly with your book idea.

POLISH YOUR COMMUNICATION SKILLS

Although the quality and significance of your data and analysis affect whether your work is accepted for publication, how you present the material can enhance—or detract from—editors' and reviewers' appreciation of your work. Many peer reviewers comment on an author's writing skills, even to the point of enumerating typos. Several detailed grammar and usage guides are available (see Gordon 1993 for a particularly entertaining example). Here we highlight a few major points you should consider when preparing your manuscript. Although all are relevant to academic writing in general, some are especially pertinent to archaeological writing.

The Style Guide Is Not Optional

Every journal adheres to a specific set of stylistic guidelines. As you prepare an article for submission to a particular journal, familiarize yourself with that journal's style and try to follow it as closely as you can. By doing so, you'll score points with the editor, and, once your article goes into production, you

Table 6.1. Types and Examples of English-language Archaeology Journals

International Archaeology Journals
American Antiquity
American Journal of Archaeology
Antiquity
Archaeologies
Historical Archaeology
International Journal of Historical Archaeology
Journal of Archaeological Research
Journal of Field Archaeology
Journal of Island and Coastal Archaeology
Journal of World Prehistory
World Archaeology

Archaeology Journals with Continental Coverage
Acta Archaeologica (Scandinavia)
African Archaeological Review
Ancient Mesoamerica
Archaeology in Oceania
Arctic Anthropology
Arqueologia Iberoamericana
Asian Perspectives
Canadian Journal of Archaeology
Eurasian Prehistory
European Journal of Archaeology
Hesperia (Mediterranean)
International Journal of South American Archaeology
Journal of African Archaeology
Journal of Caribbean Archaeology
Journal of East Asian Archaeology
Journal of Mediterranean Archaeology
Latin American Antiquity
Mexicon
Near Eastern Archaeology
North American Archaeologist
Norwegian Archaeological Review
Oxford Journal of Archaeology (Europe and Mediterranean)

Method and Theory and Specialized Journals
Archaeofauna
Archaeological Dialogues
Archaeological Prospection
Archaeometry
Current Research in the Pleistocene
Geoarchaeology
International Journal of Osteoarchaeology
Journal of Anthropological Archaeology
Journal of Archaeological Method and Theory
Journal of Archaeological Science
Journal of Social Archaeology
Rock Art Research
Vegetation History and Archaeobotany

Underwater Archaeology Journals
International Journal of Nautical Archaeology
Journal of Maritime Archaeology

Regional Archaeology Journals (North America)
Archaeology of Eastern North America
Central Plains Archaeology
Journal of California and Great Basin Anthropology
Journal of Middle Atlantic Archaeology
Journal of Northwest Anthropology
Kiva
Midcontinental Journal of Archaeology
Northeast Anthropology
Northeast Historical Archaeology
Plains Anthropologist
Southeastern Archaeology

International Anthropology Journals That Publish Archaeology Articles
American Anthropologist
Annual Review of Anthropology
Current Anthropology
Journal of Anthropological Research
Journal of Ethnobiology

Magazines
American Archaeology
Archaeology
Archaeology Southwest
Biblical Archaeology Review
British Archaeology
Current Archaeology (Britain)

Online-Only Journals
Internet Archaeology
Journal of Caribbean Archaeology
Mediterranean Archaeology and Archaeometry

might even find the copyediting process a pleasant experience. You don't have to master each and every detail of style; in fact, a lot of journals have unstated preferences of which you'll be blissfully unaware. Focusing attention on some key issues, though, will enhance your standing with an editor and, down the road, the production staff:

- Length. If journal policy states that a submission is not to exceed a certain length, respect the limit.
- Notes. Use footnotes or endnotes only if they contain material that is on topic and that has direct relevance to your discussion. If a journal doesn't allow notes, don't try to sneak them in.
- Citations and references. Make sure each citation in your article has a corresponding reference, and vice versa. Be sure to format all references according to the journal's style.

Some journals have their own in-house style sheets, whereas others follow style guides used by a broad range of publications and academic disciplines. Journal-specific style guides are often based on one of the more general authorities. AAA publications, for example, follow *The Chicago Manual of Style* (CMS 2003) in most (but not all) respects, as do SAA publications. Most archaeology journals published in the United States follow the SAA style guide, available from the society's website. Most topical and regional archaeology journals also post their style guides online.

Be aware that the U.S. and British-European approaches to style diverge in important respects. Familiarity with SAA style and CMS may not be helpful if you plan to submit to a journal based outside the United States.

Are you submitting a manuscript for publication as a monograph or book? Most publishers have guidelines but may not have a style guide as detailed as those most journals maintain. You as the author may be responsible for standardizing the manuscript's style, or the publisher might assign the task to a copy editor. Find out whose job this will be. Your best option if you will be responsible is to choose a recent book or monograph on a related topic from that publisher to use as a guide.

The Deadline: More Than a Theoretical Construct

If an editor gives you a deadline by which to submit or resubmit, meet it. And make sure you include all required material with your submission. This means that all tables, figures (photos, maps, graphs, and drawings), notes, and appendixes should accompany the manuscript.

Wordsmithery

You need not entertain, spin stories, or impress the reader with your erudition. In most publications, your job will be to clearly inform the reader what you did, how you did it, what you found, and what you think about what you found. The best way to do this job is to pare down your prose to the basics. Avoid long sentences full of embedded clauses in favor of shorter, straightforward constructions. Opt for economy. Adverbs are often expendable. And get to the point: don't waste space or try the reader's patience with unnecessary digressions that may have been fun to write or were meant to satisfy your graduate advisor.

Passive Voice

Passive voice pervades academic writing, whatever the discipline. Frequent use of the passive voice makes for dull reading; you don't want to bore your editor or peer reviewer. In addition, it lacks precision, and you don't want to confuse your editor or peer reviewer. Archaeologists tend to use the passive voice frequently because they often don't know the agents responsible for the remains they study. So archaeologists write (weakly) that *camps were relocated* from the floodplain to the uplands and that *berries were consumed* in greater abundance at one point in time than another. Even when you don't know the specific agents involved, you can still inject the active voice into your accounts of the past: Late Woodland groups, or extended families, or just plain people *moved* those camps and *ate* those berries.

Archaeologists' use of the passive voice often extends to descriptions of fieldwork, and it is even less defensible in that context. Site reports often contain statements like "Ten shovel tests were excavated through the center of the surface artifact scatter." Did this happen by magic? Did space aliens do this? If you excavated the shovel tests yourself, say so. Don't shrink from the word *I*. If a group did the work, identify the actors as *we* or *the team*.

Past Tense

For many archaeologists, the past virtually comes alive. Perhaps this accounts for the tendency of some writers to describe past events using the present tense (e.g., "By 5000 B.C., the valley's inhabitants are erecting large-scale communal structures"). Although understandable in television documentaries about ancient peoples, the present tense is inappropriate in formal writing. The last thing you want to do is jar your readers, particularly an editor or reviewer, so, when referring to the past, stick to the past tense.

You can refer to extant archaeological sites, features, artifacts, and ecofacts in the present tense: "The projectile point is 10.2 centimeters long and is ground along the base." But once a site or a feature has been destroyed, whether by a bulldozer during road construction or by you during excavation, it slips into the past and triggers the past tense.

Beyond Words

Even the most modest survey or excavation can yield large amounts of data whose efficient presentation, in many cases, requires the use of nontextual elements such as tables and graphs of various kinds. These elements shouldn't be afterthoughts or window dressing to make your work look "more scientific" but should clearly relate to and complement your text. You'll need to decide, first of all, what quantitative information supports the focus of your work and relates to your target audience, and then you'll need to decide how to present that information effectively.

Tables

Avoid the temptation to plug every number you've got into a table. Consider the example in table 6.2. The information presented in this table could be more economically conveyed in a single sentence. This table just takes up space on the page.

Likewise, avoid the temptation to try and consolidate too many disparate cases or too many informational axes into a single table. Consider the example in table 6.3. A reader should be able to scan a table and easily compare cell values. Here, because the column headings vary, the cell values aren't comparable. This is a case of three tables masquerading as one.

Graphs

The same strictures offered for tables apply to graphs. As one researcher put it, "A good graph shows data that deserve to be graphed" and "succinctly emphasizes the data, not the graph itself" (Green 2006: 620). Make your graphs as clear as possible.

Table 6.2. Metric Attributes of Projectile Points from Site X

Specimen	*Length (cm)*	*Width (cm)*
Point 1	6.3	3.7
Point 2	5.8	4.2

Table 6.3. Metric Attributes of Projectile Points from Site X

Unnotched points	*Max length (cm)*	*Max width (cm)*	*Max thickness (mm)*		
Point 1	7.2	3.3	4.0		
Point 2	7.1	3.0	5.0		
Point 3	6.8	2.9	3.0		
Notched points	*Max length*	*Max width*	*Haft width*	*Grinding on haft?*	*Max thickness*
Point 4	6.8	3.0	2.9	yes	4.0
Point 5	7.1	5.0	3.0	no	6.1
Point 6	7.2	4.0	3.3	yes	5.8
Stemmed points	*Max length*	*Stem length*	*Max width*	*Stem width*	*Max thickness*
Point 7	8.0	2.4	4.1	3.0	5.5
Point 8	8.8	3.5	3.7	2.8	5.7
Point 9	9.1	3.6	3.9	3.2	5.9

Visuals

Make sure all other figures are relevant and necessary and that they add clarity and meaning to the publication. Your favorite site photo may illustrate a presentation, but it isn't necessarily appropriate in a book or article. Most publishers will require you to obtain permission from copyright holders to publish figures that aren't your own, so be prepared to track the photographer or artist down.

BOTTOM LINE: WRITE SOMETHING GOOD AND AIM IT AT THE RIGHT TARGET

Archaeologists have a lot of publishing options. To find the best outlet for your work, field-test your paper at a conference and then decide on your goals—develop a C.V. for an academic job? contribute to regional culture history? establish yourself as an expert for consulting?—and who you want to reach. Next, find the best match between your work, your professional aspirations, and the relevant journals and publishers. Finally, make your submission as problem free as possible. Your editor, reviewers, and readers will appreciate it, and in scholarly communication, a little bit of appreciation goes a long way.

FURTHER READING

American Anthropological Association. *AAA Style Guide, 2009.* http://www.aaanet.org/publications/guidelines.cfm, accessed May 28, 2010.

Flannery, Kent V. "The Golden Marshalltown: A Parable for the Archeology of the 1980s." *American Anthropologist* 84 (1982): 265–278.

Gordon, Karen Elizabeth. *The Deluxe Transitive Vampire: The Ultimate Handbook of Grammar for the Innocent, the Eager, and the Doomed.* New York: Pantheon, 1993.

Green, Joseph. "Graphs." *Chest* 130 (2006): 620–621.

Harley, Diane, Sophia Krzys Acord, Sarah Earl-Novell, Shannon Lawrence, and C. Judson King. "Archaeology Case Study." In *Assessing the Future Landscape of Scholarly Communication: An Exploration of Faculty Values and Needs in Seven Disciplines.* Berkeley: University of California-Berkeley Center for Studies in Higher Education, 2010. http://escholarship.org/uc/cshe_fsc, accessed May 28, 2010.

Society for American Archaeology. *SAA Journal Style Guide.* N.d. http://www.saa.org/StyleGuideText/tabid/985/Default.aspx, accessed May 28, 2010.

University of Chicago Press. *The Chicago Manual of Style.* 15th edition. Chicago: University of Chicago Press, 2003.

Zimmerman, Larry J. *Presenting the Past: The Archaeologist's Toolkit.* Walnut Creek, CA: AltaMira Press, 2003.

7

Applied and Public Anthropology

Tim Wallace

In this chapter I write about some lessons gleaned from my career as an applied anthropologist and journal editor. The diverse nature of what applied and public anthropologists do means that what gets written up is also diverse. Academic publication is not the only venue for applied and public anthropologists; they must also prepare reports (so-called gray material or gray literature in the academic world) that successfully communicate the issues of the clients or groups for whom they work. Aside from reports, anthropologists often have to write persuasive pieces such as media articles or promotional work. Writing about applied research for a largely academic audience is quite different from writing for diverse audiences. Academic audiences expect more theory, more citations, and a more complicated argument to carry the narrative. Accommodating what we write to the appropriate audience can be challenging for the applied and public anthropologist, and getting published can be more complicated.

Before proceeding, I want to say a brief word about "applied" versus "public" anthropology. There have been debates over whether the words "applied" and "public" mean the same thing or refer to something different, or whether they overlap or whether one encompasses the other (see, for example, Rylko-Bauer, Singer, and van Willigen 2006; Stull 2006; Borofsky 2007; Checker 2009). Those who self-identify as applied anthropologists generally talk about clients and working for people. Those who self-identify as public anthropologists generally talk about working with people with whom they have common causes in the public issues of the day. Finally, the term "practicing anthropologist" has come to refer to an anthropologist whose professional role lies mainly outside of academia. Public anthropologists more often tend to self-identify as academic anthropologists, while applied anthropologists often have some role in an academic setting, even when their work might be for a paying client. In general, this chapter addresses anthropologists who aspire to publish as either public or applied anthropologists.

This brings us to the first lesson.

1. If you are doing applied or public anthropology work, be prepared to write well, and quickly, anytime, anywhere, regardless of the nature of the project. In the mid-1980s, I was working in Ecuador for a macro-economic policy research company. It was my first overseas consulting contract. I was flustered at the enormity of the task that lay ahead of me: to document the nature and extent of Ecuador's potato marketing system across the length and breadth of the country—in four weeks! Naively, I asked my boss, who was a Ph.D. agricultural economist, how to collect the data he wanted. His response was, "Hey, I'm an economist, you're the anthropologist, you tell me!" So I set to work, mostly on the fly, figuring out how to use rapid-assessment procedures to get the work done. It was completed on time, but I spent about half my time doing fieldwork and half the time writing the final report. It became clear that the report writing was as important as the data collection. Apparently, what I did worked, as I was hired several more times by the same company as a consultant for other projects in other countries.

Most applied and public anthropologists are more concerned with getting their work done for their clients or allies than with "getting published," but writing well is a key component of doing good applied work. This kind of work requires not only doing good fieldwork and analysis, but also convincing your readers. You have to convey successfully to those you work for what they need from you. Hence, it is imperative that you use good writing techniques, which moves us on to the second lesson.

2. Writing well is learned by practice; it does not come naturally.

> People tend to look at successful writers . . . and think they sit down at their desks every morning feeling like a million dollars, feeling great about who they are and how much talent they have. . . . Very few writers know what they are doing until they've done it. Nor do they go about their business feeling dewy-eyed and thrilled. . . . For me and most other writers I know, writing is not rapturous. In fact the only way I can get anything written at all is to write really shitty first drafts.
>
> —writer Anne Lamott

Regardless of one's identity as an applied anthropologist, a public anthropologist, or a practicing anthropologist, good writing (not to mention good research) is essential, but it is not easy, as Lamott suggests in the preceding quotation. The people you are working for—or with—depend on your writing acumen, and your future work with them and others depends on it. Writing is one of the most important skills applied anthropologists have to offer their clients. Most applied anthropologists are not hired to be good quantitative data analysts, though we can do that, too. Mostly we are employed to figure out what works and what doesn't work and then to explain why, in terms that are clear, concise, and to the point. Wordiness is not a trait appreciated by clients, or by a general audience; hence the need for well-crafted one- or two-page executive summaries to the final report on the work completed. Writing for clients and for a general audience is different from writing for colleagues in the discipline. Your prose needs to be relatively free of jargon, and you should use words that are better suited to nonspecialists.

I know from experience that it is difficult to remove the ego from one's work; thus, seek advice from mentors at the start of your writing enterprise (Wolcott 1994, 2010). They can assist in appraising which outlet is best for your work and what writing style might be suited for that outlet. Make sure you also ask them to review your work before you send off the final draft to the publication's editor. Don't be afraid of criticism, and don't take their comments personally. Their suggestions will help you produce a better draft.

Regarding outlets, there is another type of writing, one that differs from that targeted to an academic audience. I refer to journalistic work—reporting on events, public issues, and politics and opinion writing. This brings us to point number 3.

3. Applied anthropologists and especially public anthropologists need to find ways to communicate their findings and motivate for civic action. Not since Margaret Mead, who published in *Redbook* magazine and other popular venues, has there been an anthropologist so committed to regularly communicating anthropological knowledge and research to the public. But, indeed, as Brian McKenna says, "Why not turn your academic articles and books into public writing as well? After all, the hard work of research and writing the first draft has already been done" (McKenna 2010a: 12). McKenna is a former journalist turned anthropologist who teaches at the University of Michigan at Dearborn. He writes pieces not only for an academic audience, but also for the public. He believes that anthropologists seem reluctant to write for the public media. Yet that is what public anthropology should also be about.

McKenna lays out three ways to contribute your anthropological talents to the public media (2010a, 2010b). The first is by working as a *cultural broker* between academia and the general public. Here you can keep working in an academic setting but also publish journalistically. In this scenario you go from research to the public. Furthermore, you can publish an academic piece while writing another one for the media, thus fulfilling the applied anthropologist's commitment to the public. (See the Society for Applied Anthropology code of ethics [http://sfaa.net/sfaaethic.html], which in point 6 states, "We should communicate our understanding of human life to the society at large.") A second way is to take your anthropological skills and work in investigative journalism. Here one combines journalism and anthropological research into meaningful endeavors that advance the key issues of the day.

The third way McKenna suggests is to "write short (750-word), timely, journalistic pieces as a portal to influence public policy" (McKenna 2010a: 12). For example, he has composed and published more than 100 articles of this nature in his 20-year career. "Topics [of McKenna's journal pieces] have included golf courses, university pollution, wetland recovery, government corruption, the hydrogen car, school bus pollution, science museums, cool cities, the cultural history of the local lake . . . even how the local weather forecast is ideological" (McKenna 2010a: 12). Journalistic pieces informed by social and anthropological research are often collaborative and dynamic, wherein the journalism is improved by the anthropology and the anthropology responds to the needs of the people being affected by the social issues under scrutiny. Theory and knowledge can be advanced by investigative work that is done as part of and in connection with the key social issues of the day (see Hale 2008). So, moving on to lesson 4, let me discuss the value of professional and public newsletters.

4. Non-peer-reviewed outlets are a good way to get your ideas out quickly and in press. Newsletters and similar outlets are not peer reviewed but have large readership and can be a great way to get practice writing and get your ideas before a lot of people, including nonacademic readers.

For example, in the spring of 2011, I served as editor of the Society for Applied Anthropology's *SfAA News*. The *SfAA News* has a circulation of about 3,500 and more online. The SfAA prides itself on being interdisciplinary. The *SfAA News*, in four issues a year, publishes a wide range of articles and commentaries, as perusal of a recent issue will attest (see "Resources" at the end of the chapter). Although the *SfAA News* is not peer reviewed, it is widely read and is a good vehicle for getting your ideas or applied research in print. Just e-mail the editor by consulting the link to get the ball rolling. There are usually several student-written pieces every issue, and the editor is always looking for more students to write for the newsletter.

Practicing Anthropology is a non-peer-reviewed journal published by the SfAA. It was started at the University of South Florida in 1978. It publishes quarterly and is editor reviewed rather than peer reviewed. Only the editors decide which articles to use, instead of having colleagues review them first and make recommendations to the editors. This journal is aimed at anthropologists working outside academia who may not have as much time to digest long, theory-laden articles. Instead, the editors select shorter, practical pieces that keep both jargon and citations to a minimum.

Another newsletter-type possibility is that of the National Association for the Practice of Anthropology (NAPA). NAPA is a section of the American Anthropological Association (AAA). With approximately 600 members, it is one of the larger sections in the AAA. Like the *SfAA News*, it is also an important venue for getting your ideas and work out quickly and effectively. One can also write a column in the NAPA section of the AAA's *Anthropology News*. Many students have published short articles there (fewer than 1,000 words). The person to contact is the NAPA secretary, whose address can be located at the NAPA website.

Blogging might be another way to get ideas widely dispersed. NAPA's website (http://practicinganthropology.org) is an excellent place to submit a blog post. There are other options for blog posts, too. The March 2010 issue of *American Anthropologist* includes a review essay written by David Price (2010: 140–142) and discusses blogging, especially *Savage Minds*, *Zero Anthropology*, and *AAA Blog*, among others.

Each of these professional newsletters and sites represent opportunities for you to present your ideas and findings. But there are other public options as well, where you will have a more diverse audience. Recently, a number of public and applied anthropologists have been sending their work to *Counterpunch*, an online political newsletter; others submit blog posts to the *Huffington Post*. These sites have wide readership, including many people who do not identify as anthropologists.

Finally, make sure you explore opportunities at your own university. Almost every university has an alumni magazine or an official bulletin and perhaps even a press department. Try them. Your own academic department probably has a newsletter, or you can create one. This is how the Kroeber Anthropological Society (KAS) Papers started. Dating from 1949, the KAS is a graduate student–organized project at the University of California at Berkeley and is the oldest such organization in the United States. The papers they publish are outstanding and well recognized. There is every reason to get a newsletter started in your own department, even if the circulation is small. It serves as another place to get experience writing for a professional audience.

While newsletters, newspapers, and blogs are ways to write for a more general audience and good experience for those who want to disseminate their ideas and practical applied work, let us remember the importance of the traditional means of publishing in academia, which leads us to the next lesson.

5. Publishing in journals with a more applied focus is rewarding, too, but the demands on the author are much greater and the process takes much longer. There are not as many peer-reviewed publications that are explicitly outlets for applied and public anthropology as there are for general academic anthropology. In many countries anthropologists don't even make the distinction between applied and nonapplied anthropology (Baba and Hill 2006: 177). Especially outside North America and Western Europe, anthropologists receive classic anthropology training, but with the absence of academic jobs that pay sufficiently to support a family, many foreign anthropologists work for nongovernmental organizations (NGOs) and governmental entities doing applied work to supplement their income. Thus, in many countries the distinction between academic and applied is not significant, and this carries over to publications. In Guatemala, for example, Ph.D. anthropologists and students publish in the same journals, in part because students gather the data, and the Ph.D. anthropologists organize and oversee the research (see, for example, Bastos and Cumes 2007). Even in the United Kingdom, applied anthropology as a separate field has had only spotty acceptance from professionals in the broader discipline (Pink 2006).

In the United States, the principal peer-reviewed journals in applied and public anthropology, in my opinion, are *Human Organization*, the flagship journal of the SfAA, and the *Annals of Anthropological Practice* (previously known as the *NAPA Bulletin*), the main publication of the National Association for the Practice of Anthropology.

Human Organization (*HO*) is the oldest and most widely recognized journal in applied anthropology. It has been published continuously since 1941. Its citation rate is among the highest as compared to scientific anthropology journals (Griffith 2008: 51). All scholarly journals include information about how to submit on the inside of their front cover; alternatively you can find the websites for these publications in the "Resources" section.

HO's current editor (personal communication) reports that there is a quick turnaround for review of submitted manuscripts, but it is extremely rare for a manuscript to be accepted for publication without going through at least one round of "revise and resubmit." Among academically situated applied anthropologists, publication in *HO* is seen as a feather in one's professional cap. Furthermore, since the SfAA is an international and interdisciplinary organization, there is a steady stream of manuscripts coming from scholars outside the discipline and outside the United States.

In general, only the highest-quality manuscripts make it through the peer-review process. If you want to submit your work to *HO*, make sure you have had a colleague or mentor read it before submission. The content of your article must contain some theory as well as the main issue you want to present. The editors, like SfAA members in general, have a strong scientific focus, so other paradigms, theoretical approaches, or unusual, non-hypothesis-driven methodologies may be less readily accepted. But don't get discouraged. Every time you get a revise-and-resubmit or a rejection, you also get more constructive feedback about how to improve your manuscript for the next time. Absorb what the reviewers tell you and rewrite. Again, you cannot let reviewers' criticism become personal. Learn from your mistakes and edit a new, improved draft of your manuscript.

The *Annals of Anthropological Practice* is a much newer journal. The first issue came out in 1985, not long after NAPA was formed as a section with the 1983 reorganization of the AAA. When the SfAA broke its close ties with the AAA to become a separate organization, NAPA was born to ensure that the applied perspective remained vital within the organization. Its content is peer reviewed, and it accepts individual submissions as well as thematic collections.

American Anthropologist publishes across the spectrum of anthropology, including practicing and applied research. Another possible outlet for your more academic articles is *Anthropology in Action: Journal for Applied Anthropology in Policy and Action*. Published in the United Kingdom by Berghahn since 2005, in connection with the Association for Anthropology in Action, this journal is a relatively new one, with three issues a year. You might also consider *Collaborative Anthropologies*, the brainchild of Luke Eric Lassiter, whose books and articles on the topic have put him at the forefront of thinking about how anthropologists collaborate with the people they study or for whom they work. This is a very new journal—the first issue was published in 2008—and is published by the University of Nebraska Press. There is only one issue per year. But if you are interested in writing about your collaborative research or activist work, this may be just the journal for you.

6. The real craft of writing is in the editing, so become an assistant editor and learn how.

> Good writing is essentially rewriting.
>
> —author Roald Dahl

> When I say writing, O believe me, it is rewriting that I have chiefly in mind.
>
> —novelist Robert Louis Stevenson

I was the editor for the *NAPA Bulletin* from 2004 to 2009 and found it to be a very interesting, enjoyable, and rewarding professional experience. As an editor as well for the *SfAA News* (2008–2011), I learned that clear, concise, yet engaging writing has been an essential element in my editing. In both cases, I found well-known authors writing bad prose, and student authors writing very good prose, but in general, the more writing experience one has, the better one's writing is.

Although carving out the first draft may be the hardest part of the writing process, it really is in the editing where the real crafting takes place. I suggest some resources in the "Further Reading" section.

One more piece of advice: never be stubborn about holding on to a specific phrase or paragraph, or even whole sections. Let them go if your mentor tells you they don't fit. Unfortunately, many authors fail to do a good editing job before submitting their manuscript for review. Sometimes a good manuscript is much better without that paragraph you think is wonderful. Poorly edited drafts hurt you, the author, because the import of what is being said is lost on the reader, even if your words get published.

Becoming an assistant editor yourself is a good means by which you can quickly gain knowledge about how to get published. For example, the Student Committee of the SfAA has a newsletter editor who solicits pieces from student SfAA members, edits them, and readies them for each issue of *SfAA News*. The *Annals of Anthropological Practice* does not have any student editors, but students work for the editors as assistants. There is a student member of the NAPA Publications Committee (which is also true for the SfAA).

And so we come to the end of the lessons. Oh! There is one more, and I borrow it from Harry Wolcott's book (1994: 41) on transforming qualitative research into publishable tracts:

7. "When you come to the end, stop! Take the account as far as you can with confidence, then stop while ahead."

FURTHER READING

Baba, Marietta, and Carole E. Hill. "What's in the Name 'Applied Anthropology'? An Encounter with Global Practice." *NAPA Bulletin* 25, no. 1 (2006): 176–207.

Bastos, Santiago, and Aura Cumes. *Mayanizacion y Vida Cotidiana, V. II: Los Estudios de Caso*. Guatemala: FLACSO-CIRMA-Cholsamaj, 2007.

Borofsky, Robert. "Public Anthropology: A Personal Perspective." 2007. http://www.marshall.edu/coll-anth/index.html.

Checker, Melissa. "Anthropology in the Public Sphere, 2008: Emerging Trends and Significant Events." *American Anthropologist* 111, no. 2 (2009): 162–169.

Checker, Melissa, David Vine, and Alaka Wali. "A Sea Change in Anthropology? Public Anthropology Reviews." *American Anthropologist* 112, no. 1 (2010): 5–6.

Griffith, David. "From the *Human Organization* Editors' Desk." *SfAA Newsletter* 19, no. 3 (August 2008): 51–52.

Hale, Charles R., ed. *Engaging Contradictions: Theory, Politics, and Methods of Activist Scholarship*. Berkeley: University of California Press, 2008.

Kedia, Satish, and David Himmelgreen. "From the Editors of the *NAPA Bulletin*." *American Anthropologist* 111, no. 2 (2009): 135–136.

Lamott, Anne. *Bird by Bird*. New York: Random House, 1994.

McKenna, Brian. "Doing Anthropology as an Environmental Journalist: Tales and Tips, Part 1." *SfAA News* 21, no. 2 (May 2010a): 11–14.

McKenna, Brian. "Anthropology Must Embrace Journalism: Public Pedagogy Is Discipline's Challenge." *Tsantsa* 15 (2010b): 47–60.

Pink, Sarah. "The Practice of Anthropology in Great Britain." *NAPA Bulletin* 25, no. 1 (2006): 123–133.

Price, David. "Blogging Anthropology: Savage Minds, Zero Anthropology, and AAA Blogs." *American Anthropologist* 112, no. 1 (March 2010): 140–142.

Rylko-Bauer, Barbara, Merrill Singer, and John van Willigen. "Rethinking Applied Anthropology: Its Past, Present and Future."*American Anthropologist* 108, no. 1 (2006): 178–190.

Stull, Donald. "President's Letter." *SfAA Newsletter* 17, no. 2 (May 2006): 1–3.

Wolcott, Harry F. *Transforming Qualitative Data: Description, Analysis and Interpretation*. Thousand Oaks, CA: Sage, 1994.

Wolcott, Harry F. *Ethnography Lessons: A Primer*. Walnut Creek, CA: Left Coast Press, 2010.

Zinsser, William. *On Writing Well, 30th Anniversary Edition: The Classic Guide to Writing Non-Fiction*. New York: Harper Paperbacks, 2006.

RESOURCES

Non-peer-reviewed outlets

NAPA e-Newsletter
http://practicinganthropology.org

Practicing Anthropology
http://sfaa.net/pa/pa.html

SfAA News
http://sfaa.net/newsletter/newsletter.html

Blogs

AAA Blog
http://blog.aaanet.org

Savage Minds
http://savageminds.org

Zero Anthropology
http://zeroanthropology.net

Journals

Annals of Anthropological Practice
http://www.wiley.com/bw/journal.asp?ref=1556-4789&site=1

Anthropology in Action: Journal for Applied Anthropology in Policy and Action
http://www.berghahnbooks.com/journals/aia/index.php

Collaborative Anthropologies
http://www.marshall.edu/coll-anth/index.html

Human Organization
http://www.sfaa.net/ho/main/author.html

8

Biological and Physical Anthropology

Paul A. Garber

In our roles as educators and researchers, biological anthropology graduate students and faculty are called on to conduct research that contributes new knowledge to our individual fields of study and offers new theoretical insights that advance our discipline. The challenges of conducting scientific research (i.e., formulating a clear set of testable hypotheses, developing an appropriate methodology to examine these hypotheses, and analyzing the results), however, are formidable and require an enormous effort in time and creativity. The mentoring I received in graduate school and in working with colleagues prepared me well for the tasks of producing and analyzing results. However, I found myself less knowledgeable and somewhat intimidated by the final step in this process, namely disseminating new information and ideas to the public and scientific communities through scholarly publications. Although there was no shortage of journal articles and book chapters to read or refer to as examples, I had no real understanding of the processes of manuscript preparation, submission, peer review, and publication.

This chapter is designed to provide a helpful discussion of strategies for publishing in biological anthropology. In this subdiscipline, the two primary activities are presenting research at conferences and, above all, publishing research reports in journals. The bulk of this chapter addresses practical tips for how to write a publishable scientific paper, how to select an appropriate journal, and for determining when it is best to publish your work as a journal article, book chapter, or book-length manuscript, or as part of a special issue of a research journal or as a web production.

JOURNALS

Constructing a clear and straightforward argument to examine a set of research questions can be an extremely rewarding personal and intellectual experience. Seeing your ideas in print or online (or, before e-books and digital journals, in a volume on the library shelf) and your research cited as providing empirical support for a new theoretical perspective is exciting. However, writing is hard work; it requires many drafts and at times can be frustrating. In sitting down to write, one is best advised to heed the words of Wonderland's Cheshire Cat whose response to Alice's question of which road to take was, "That depends a good deal on where you want to get to." Similarly, until you have reached the point at which you fully understand your data and have a clear sense of the main conclusions and contributions of your work, the journey you take in moving from an introduction to methods to results to discussion to conclusion will be filled with false starts, recrossed paths, detours, and roadblocks.

General Advice

Publishing is an essential component of each research project. You need to put as much effort into the process of publishing as you expend developing a research project and collecting and analyzing the data. You want to be successful at publishing. If the results of your research are not available to the scientific community, then it is as if the work was never completed. As you write your article, keep your prose clear and simple. Provide examples, pay attention to detail, and avoid jargon.

Here are some specific ideas that will help you in this effort:

- Publishing is a creative process. It can take considerable time and thought, many, many drafts, and the courage to modify and develop existing ideas.
- Consider your title and keywords carefully. As both the title of your manuscript and the keywords following the abstract are used for indexing and literature searches, these should be chosen carefully to highlight the major contribution of the published work and to help interested researchers locate your contribution to scholarship. Generally, you want to think about groups of researchers who would be interested in your findings and propose terms that align with how they might look up information.
- Locate some cold readers to test that your prose is clear and that your arguments make sense. Have colleagues, even some not in your field, critically read and comment on your manuscript before you decide it is ready to submit for review and publication.

Selecting an Appropriate Journal

Biological anthropologists are expected to publish the majority of their research in nationally and internationally recognized journals such as the *American Journal of Physical Anthropology*, the *Journal of Human Evolution*, the *American Journal of Primatology*, the *International Journal of Primatology*, *Current Anthropology*, *American Anthropologist*, and *Human Biology*, as well as in a set of journals that are read principally by a smaller and highly targeted audience in your specific field of study.

In selecting the most appropriate journal for your manuscript, there are several factors to consider, including the readership of the journal, whether the journal is peer reviewed, the impact factor of the journal, and the journal's time from submission to publication. Information like this is posted online by the journal publishers.

As a graduate student or a recent Ph.D., having one or even two journal articles published is a critical first step in advancing your career. Thus, timing merits additional comment. Although journal editors and reviewers work extremely hard to move manuscripts through the submission process, journals vary in time to publication. With some journals, articles appear online within 3 to 4 weeks of acceptance and are available in print within 5 to 6 months of acceptance. In the case of other journals, an article may not appear in print for 12 to 18 months. Most journals include information on the first page of each published article indicating the date the manuscript was received and the date the manuscript was accepted, or you can e-mail the editor and ask about average time to publication.

For junior scholars who are applying for academic positions or are scheduled to be evaluated for promotion, time to publication is an especially important factor. There is an important courtesy that you must follow: your article may be under consideration with only one journal at a time. Plan ahead. The time it takes to publish is longer than you think, particularly as your top pick or two might decline to publish the paper.

The second most important consideration in journal selection is the evaluation or ranking based on the journal title's impact factor. The impact factor (sometimes also called "IF") is a measure over the course of two years of the average number of times each published article was cited in an indexed journal. For example, in 2008, the *Journal of Human Evolution* had an impact factor of 3.55, and the *American Journal of Physical Anthropology* had an impact factor of 2.35. In 2009, the journal *Science* had an impact factor of 29.70. There currently exist some 8,000 indexed journals, and the impact factor of each of these journals is listed in the *Journal Citation Reports* (http://thomsonreuters.com/products_services/science/science_products/a-z/journal_citation_reports).

It is considered more prestigious to publish in journals with higher impact factors, because they contain articles that are widely cited by scholars. I would recommend targeting your strongest publications to journals that have an impact factor of 1.50 or greater. Some hiring and promotion committees will ask candidates to provide the impact factors for the journal articles listed on their C.V., so publishing in high-impact journals is an important accomplishment for young scholars.

As mentioned, most journals insist that your article be under submission with only one journal at a time (because editors don't want to waste their or their reviewers' time on manuscripts that may end up being published elsewhere). Thus, you will need to create a prioritized list and seek the advice of colleagues in your field concerning the sequence of publication venues. Given the widespread availability of journal articles in both print and downloadable forms, journals that are available digitally represent the most effective way for sharing information among biological anthropologists.

Submitting to the Selected Journal

Virtually all journals use an online submission system. Such websites make it relatively easy to provide the required author information and upload the text, tables, and figures for your manuscript. As a journal editor, I offer two very simple suggestions when submitting your manuscript. First, read the information provided in the instructions to authors carefully. Make certain that your manuscript is formatted correctly (different journals use different formatting and referencing styles) and adheres to all provisos required for publishing in that journal. Second, before you complete the final stage of the submission process, carefully review the system-generated PDF version of your manuscript to make certain that all parts of your manuscript, including tables and figures, have been compiled correctly. Failure to do either of these steps will result in a delay as the manuscript will be sent back to you for proper formatting and resubmission.

You should send your manuscript to a journal whose mission statement (usually included on the inside cover of the journal or in the instructions to authors) fits well with the research and theoretical framework presented in your article. You might consider submitting your work to journals cited in your list of references. A good rule of thumb is to submit your strongest manuscripts to the official or flagship journal of one of the major professional societies to which you are a member. As stated, be aware that professional ethics and journal procedures require that you submit your manuscript to only one journal at a time. Editors spend a lot of time and resources on submissions, and they do not want to find out that this time was superfluous because the manuscript will be published elsewhere. If your manuscript is rejected or deemed unsuitable for publication in a particular journal, then and only then can you revise, reformat, and submit your manuscript to another journal for publication.

A quick word about what happens to your article once you hit "submit" and send forth your manuscript into the electronic submission system: Your article will likely be sent out for a reading by other topical experts in a process called "peer review." Peer review is a critical part of the evaluation process, and it relies on the expertise of scholars in your field who are invited to critically evaluate the quality, impact, and contribution of your manuscript. Although we all dread having our work critiqued, the reviewers are giving freely of their time and experience to help you, the author, transform a good manuscript into an even stronger scientific contribution.

Although peer-reviewed journals differ in the exact details of the review process, in general, each manuscript is evaluated by two or three external reviewers. Based on this information, you will likely receive a decision letter that outlines the strengths and weaknesses of your manuscript within the context of the comments of the reviewers. In most high-impact journals, well over 50% of the manuscripts submitted are rejected. Even the strongest scholars in your field have had several of their manuscripts rejected; you just don't see their rejections. Take heart that they don't see your rejections either. Having your manuscript rejected does not mean that the research should remain unpublished. Manuscripts are rejected for many reasons, including the fact that your subject matter may not be appropriate or of sufficient interest to the readership of that journal, the data set presented may be judged to be too preliminary, a reviewer may think the results do not strongly support your conclusions but may in fact support an alternative set of conclusions, or, in its present form, the manuscript may contain serious flaws and require rethinking.

In the lucky happenstance that you are asked to revise and resubmit your manuscript, do not groan. This is a wonderful compliment, and it is essential to respond to each of the reviewers' comments individually and provide a detailed description of the specific changes made (including line numbers of the revised text). In some instances you may disagree with the comments of a reviewer. The reviewer may have misunderstood the text, but the comment suggests that your writing was unclear and that you need to revise the manuscript in such a way as to avoid the ambiguity. If you think, however, that the reviewer's argument is incorrect, write a justification in which you present a defense of your position. Again, remember that the reviewers and journal editor are offering their time and expertise to help you strengthen your manuscript and that this is high praise.

Whether you agree or disagree with the specifics, pay careful attention to reviewers' comments. Manuscripts that are revised and resubmitted are generally sent back to the original reviewers for a second evaluation, which means that only papers that thoughtfully responded to reviewers' concerns are likely to be accepted. If your paper is not ultimately accepted, it will still benefit from these efforts. Keep in mind that your next journal may send your manuscript (by accident) to the same reviewer. You want to refine your article to demonstrate engagement with the reviewer's concerns.

Organizing a Special Issue

A more ambitious publication strategy that recent Ph.D.s might consider involves organizing a symposium for a national or international meeting, with the goal of having all of the papers published together as a special issue of a journal. This requires identifying and bringing together an appropriate set of scholars to present new data and perspectives on a particular topic, taxon, or theoretical issue. Although this may seem a bit intimidating to young scholars (a junior scholar could partner with a more senior scholar so that both share the responsibilities of serving as guest editors for the special issue), it is an opportunity for them to bring visibility to themselves and their research.

Assuming that the symposium is successful and well received, the next step is to select an appropriate journal, write a brief prospectus outlining the goals of the special issue and including paper titles and author(s)' affiliations, and send this to the journal editor. The advantages of organizing a special issue of a peer-reviewed journal are many. First, your name and your manuscript will be featured along with other outstanding scholars in a single, widely read and widely cited journal issue. Since authors have already presented their contribution at the symposium, it is reasonable to have them submit their final manuscript to the journal within a few months. Although each article is reviewed and evaluated by the journal on its own merit, it is my experience that special issues are of great interest to journal editors and appear in print in a more timely fashion than edited books.

General Advice for Developing a Special Issue of a Journal

- When organizing the original symposium, poll contributors to determine interest in submitting their manuscript as part of a special issue of a journal.
- Have contributors bring two hard copies of their presentation with them to the symposium. As symposium organizer, you should review the manuscripts and distribute the second copies to one of the other symposium

participants for a second review. These in-house reviews will help authors prepare and strengthen their manuscripts for publication.
- Work with contributing authors and the journal editor to develop a realistic timetable for manuscript submission and a tentative publication date.

BOOK-LENGTH WORKS

Book chapters represent another important publication venue in biological anthropology. Given that senior colleagues are usually invited to submit a chapter for an edited volume, it is highly prestigious when young scholars are asked to do so.

There are several advantages to writing a book chapter. First, book chapters are often written in a more engaging style, include a more expansive review of the literature, address a broader set of questions, and offer a greater opportunity to speculate beyond the narrow constraints of the data than is permitted in a journal article. In addition, chapters in a book follow a single or related set of themes, so having your chapter alongside chapters written by well-respected figures in the field elevates your visibility as a young scholar.

The disadvantages of writing a chapter for an edited volume are that since the editor(s) has a strong interest in including your chapter in the volume, book chapters are often less rigorously reviewed and are therefore perceived by promotion and academic review committees to carry less weight and scholarly impact than publishing in a peer-reviewed journal. Two other limitations of publishing book chapters are that (a) they almost always take several years to publish (if there are 20 contributors, the volume does not go to the publisher until all chapters are completed) and (b) books chapters are less accessible and more difficult to find in online searches (although this reality may change with e-books) than are journal articles.

The publication of a book-length manuscript is considerably more common among cultural anthropologists and archaeologists than among biological anthropologists. Biological anthropologists rely on the mores established in the biological sciences and, as such, are encouraged to publish the results of their doctoral dissertation and subsequent research as a series of journal articles and chapters in edited volumes. Certainly in terms of obtaining an academic position or promotion from assistant to associate professor, biological anthropologists are rarely required to have published a single-author book and are likely to be evaluated based on the prestige of the journals that have accepted their research article publications.

MULTIMEDIA PROJECTS

More and more scholars are engaging each other and the public using blogs and other forms of online communication. It is my experience that many departments and faculty have not yet considered how these new forms of information exchange should be valued. For example, should blog posts be considered as public engagement and service or as some form of scholarly presentation (like presenting a poster at a local conference)? Clearly, as blog posts and tweets are not peer reviewed, they are unlikely to be considered as a form of scholarly publication. That said, young scholars who maintain high-quality blogs may emerge as leading voices in ongoing intellectual debates. I would caution, however, that writers of blog posts and tweets have an obligation to identify their personal beliefs and biases as distinct from scientific evidence and factual information, as their words may end up being cited in reports and publications.

You may also wish to consult the introduction to this volume, which includes a discussion of "prior publication." In biological journals, announcing research findings, even as abstracts, can mean prior publication and can jeopardize your ability to publish the research results in a peer-reviewed journal, a situation that could greatly set back a junior scholar.

FINAL THOUGHTS

Science is a collaborative process in which we communicate and exchange ideas and information. We accomplish this in the classroom, in public lectures and presentations at conferences, and in publishing the results of our research. Writing a publishable manuscript is a challenging but highly rewarding experience that advances our field of study and stimulates new research and ideas. The hardest part of writing is getting started. Many of us clean our house, write letters, bake cookies, or perform other procrastinating rituals before we can sit down at the computer and begin drafting a manuscript. However, publishing is essential to science, and securing academic positions requires that this activity be robustly evident on your C.V.

Once you begin the writing process, your ideas will flow. Before submitting a manuscript for publication, seek the advice of colleagues and ask them to read and comment on your work. Present your ideas at conferences and seminars to obtain feedback for rethinking your arguments and conclusions. Once you submit your manuscript, use the input you receive from journal editors and peer reviewers to strengthen the contribution of your manuscript to the discipline.

FURTHER READING

Anderson, Greg. "How to Write a Paper in Scientific Journal Style and Format." Bates College, 2004. http://abacus.bates.edu/~ganderso/biology/resources/writing/HTWtoc.html, accessed April 1, 2011.

Day, Robert A., and Barbara Gastel. *How to Write and Publish a Scientific Paper*. 6th edition. Westport, CT: Greenwood Press, 2006.

Kelner, Katrina. "Tips for Publishing in Scientific Journals." *Science Careers*, April 6, 2007. doi:10.1126/science.caredit.a0700046.

RESOURCES

Nature offers a collection of articles about peer review and its limitations:
http://www.nature.com/nature/peerreview/debate/index.html

This library web page suggests that prospective authors look up journals in Ulrich's Periodical Directory Online:
http://www.lib.utexas.edu/lsl/help/modules/peer.html

9

Cultural/Social Anthropology and Ethnography

Catherine Besteman

Ethnography is the seminal contribution and backbone of sociocultural anthropology. For most sociocultural anthropologists, ethnography provides the basis of almost everything we do as scholars, from pedagogy to publishing, theory to policy. This chapter offers practical advice for how to develop your ethnographic knowledge into a form for dissemination within and beyond the academy.

Whether presented as a linear narrative, case studies, poetic fragments, anecdotes and quotations, life histories, reflexive engagement, or something else, the point of ethnography is to keep human experience at the heart of the text, to present a compelling portrait or argument, to construct a story that is meaningful and accessible, and to contribute toward building theories of human life. Ethnography is anthropology's most powerful way to tell, translate, analyze, and critique human experience. Although this chapter is more about how to plan a publishing trajectory than how to write, it is worth noting that one can strive to write ethnography that is captivating as well as edifying.

PLANNING A PUBLICATION TRAJECTORY

After the dissertation is finished, the process of sharing your ethnographic knowledge and theoretical contributions more broadly begins in earnest. The primary place to start is to identify your desired audience and then choose the venue and format for the greatest impact. Sociocultural anthropologists write for various audiences, including fellow academics and specialists, students, policy makers, the community in which they live, the community about which they write, local and transnational advocacy and activist groups, interested nonspecialists and the general reading public, and journalists and pundits. Often these categories overlap. (One can think of other audiences that raise particular ethical questions, such as tourists, certain corporations, and the military.)

Identifying your desired audience requires that you know what your point is and, obviously, for whom you are writing. What is the value of your ethnographic knowledge? Who will benefit from it? What impact do you wish to make? Do you have theoretical aspirations to use your ethnographic knowledge to build or refine models of human societies, behaviors, and perceptions? Do you wish to impact policy and effect social change? Are your aims more lyrical or phenomenological—to turn ethnography toward literary poetics or empathetic understanding? Or perhaps your top priority is simply pedagogical—to contribute, as Clifford Geertz once put it, to the sum total of what was said? Do you wish to create an archive for posterity or for legal claims, perhaps in collaboration with the community in which you work? Whether your concern is theoretical, activist, literary, pedagogical, documentary, or some combination, there is a publication venue for you. The trick is to find the appropriate outlet and form, as well as to understand the best balance of publications for getting your first job and, if in the academy, receiving tenure.

Identifying your target audience and defining your central point help determine the best publication venue. For example, if your goal is to impact health care policy, an article in a specialist anthropology journal is not the best choice. If your goal is to get tenure *and* impact health care policy, then you might wish to publish a theoretical piece in a peer-reviewed anthropology journal and, in addition, place an op-ed in a newspaper and work with an advocacy group to write a policy brief for elected representatives and other interested people.

For academic positions in anthropology, peer-reviewed academic journals and sole-authored books with respected publishers still remain the gold standard for tenure decisions. Most academic departments seek candidates who have published journal articles. Some departments are increasingly recognizing the value and importance of crossover publications that speak to audiences outside the academy. Plan your publication trajectory in dialogue with senior faculty in your department and in conjunction with a review of the evaluation standards at your university or college. These two things should advise you about the specific balance expected of journal articles, books, conference papers, and other forms of publication, including websites, op-eds, popular essays, and collaborative and advocacy work with nonacademics.

For tenure, some departments will expect several peer-reviewed journal articles and conference presentations; some will also expect evidence of a book manuscript; and some will require journal articles, presentations, and a completed book, preferably with published reviews. In general, it is wise to submit several articles to peer-reviewed journals while working on your book manuscript. The criticism you receive from journal reviewers will strengthen your book manuscript as well, and published journal articles are essential if your book manuscript is still under review or in press when you come up for tenure.

Along the way you will probably be asked to write book reviews for anthropology journals. Among other things, writing book reviews is a good way to practice writing concisely, but as they can be quite time consuming, try to impose a time limit of three days spent on each review. Book reviews provide evidence in your tenure case of service to the discipline but generally are not treated as equivalent to publications.

The discussion here offers suggestions about shaping your ethnographic writing for different kinds of publications.

JOURNALS

Journal articles are the vehicles for introducing your work to an academic audience. From the dissertation you have a wealth of fine-grained ethnographic knowledge, a thorough command of the literature relevant to your subject, and new theoretical contributions to the discipline. Journal articles offer you the opportunity to tease out and develop individual parts of your dissertation research for slightly different audiences (such as the "journal triangle" approach suggested by Boellstorff in chapter 4).

Think of journal articles as individual gems, each containing its own structure, luster, sparkle, and impact. Each article should be crafted independently around a central point or argument. Clearly define for yourself exactly what that point/argument is before you start writing and remind yourself of it often while you write. Stay focused, don't ramble, resist tangents (but make a note of them for future articles), and don't get lost in irrelevant details or excessive posturing.

Some scholars suggest treating journal articles as the building blocks of a book manuscript by envisioning each article as a book chapter. Since in that case the articles would have to be heavily revised to ensure consistency and narrative flow, you could, alternatively, use journal articles to develop different components or themes of your book manuscript. Journal articles can also be outlets for dissertation material that is interesting and meaningful but not relevant to the book you are writing from your dissertation research.

Do not attempt to condense your entire dissertation into one or even two articles. The result is usually messy, sprawling, and unfocused. Rather, choose several particular points that you think are important contributions to the literature and develop each with a clear, focused, well-researched, ethnographically supported argument.

In general, in peer-reviewed journal articles, ethnography is used to buttress a theoretical argument rather than as a stand-alone descriptive story. The ethnographic component of your article might be in the form of a traditional extended case study (thus producing a sort of "theory sandwich," where you introduce your argument, review the literature, provide the case study, and conclude with your theoretical insights). Alternatively, your ethnographic information could take the form of illustrative vignettes and anecdotes provided alongside your theoretical points, a life history that illustrates your theoretical argument, or a series of reflexive insights that provoke theoretical inspiration. Whatever structure you define for your article, remember to use your ethnographic knowledge to show rather than tell. Great ethnography speaks for itself, so let it work for you to illustrate your theoretical points.

Finally, journal articles help establish your reputation for theory and ethnography, so it is helpful to conceive of each article as a demonstration of the relationship you have developed between theory and ethnography for a particular topic. For example, an article might use a theoretical paradigm to make sense of an ethnographic account or might offer ethnographic information to develop, tweak, or debunk a theoretical argument. External reviewers for your tenure case will be asked to describe your specific contributions to the discipline, and your journal articles will be their road map.

BOOK-LENGTH WORKS

Books offer the greatest opportunity for sharing ethnographic information and developing theoretical arguments. Unfortunately, libraries are filled with boring and poorly written ethnographies, so try to keep your writing vivid, intimate, accessible, and persuasive, not tedious, pedantic, or self-aggrandizing.

Decide on your audience and write with them consistently in mind (remembering that few publishers are interested in narrowly specialized books). Anthropology should be fascinating, engrossing, and educational. It offers critical insights into (what some like to call) the human condition, so keep your language lively and clear. Avoid posturing statements like "It is my contention that . . ." and "I would like to suggest that . . . ." Also avoid filling your narrative with equivocating statements ("It seems likely to be the case that . . ."), even if you are struggling with assuming the voice of authority.

Edited volumes typically carry far less weight in tenure considerations than sole-authored books, even though they represent an enormous time commitment (not just because of editing demands but also because of the sheer amount of time it will take to communicate with each contributor about deadlines, revisions, galley reviews, references, artwork, copyrights, etc.). If, after lots of resistance, you get pulled into editing a book before writing your own, try to make your editorial commitment work for you by simultaneously teaching a course on the same topic or ensuring that the edited volume contributes to your intellectual work on your sole-authored book manuscript.

CONFERENCES

Conference presentations are important on your C.V. (your academic resume) to demonstrate your participation in a community of scholars, and most successful job candidates have paper presentations on their C.V. At the time you come up for tenure, be aware that conference papers do not count as publications in tenure considerations. In addition to networking with fellow scholars and publishers, the point of presenting at a conference is (1) to share your ideas with and receive feedback from an interested audience, (2) to help other scholars become acquainted with your research and to learn about the current research of other scholars in your area, (3) to develop ideas for future articles or book chapters, and (4) to learn how to concisely articulate your research.

In your conference presentation, have a central point and say only what you need to in order to get your point across. Don't try to squeeze so much material into your paper that you're reading at breakneck speed, and don't pepper your presentation with remarks like, "The next section of the paper talks about X, Y, and Z, but I don't have time to read it here."

Conference presentations are opportunities to take intellectual risks, float ideas, ask questions of the audience and fellow panelists, and figure out what is really novel and exciting about your work so that you can use those insights for developing publishable material.

MULTIMEDIA PROJECTS

Few young anthropologists expect to write only for academic audiences, which is a very good thing. This section offers suggestions and advice for writing beyond the academy. Since there is growing pressure for tenure reviews to include greater consideration of "public" or "engaged" anthropology, discuss your plans for developing your work in this area with senior members of your faculty if you wish to advocate for its inclusion in your review. It will be important to ensure that at least some of your external reviewers respect and appreciate this dimension of anthropology.

If your work is relevant to a current political issue or event, consider submitting an op-ed or editorial to your local newspaper (you can also try the major newspapers with national reach, but your chances of publication are smaller). Op-ed essays are usually limited to about 800 words, although editorials might be longer. Read previously published op-eds for examples of style, such as persuasive, factual, or emotionally provocative material (see Roberto Gonzalez's compilation of editorials by anthropologists, *Anthropologists in the Public Sphere*, 2004). When your essay is published, be sure to inform your university or college's communications office as well as the American Anthropological Association.

If your work is pertinent to policy considerations, consider writing (perhaps in collaboration with relevant advocacy organizations) very concise policy briefs that summarize in one page your primary policy suggestions and sending these to elected officials and pundits in the print media as well as TV, radio, and Internet sites. You might also wish to submit testimony for congressional hearings on the topic. Additionally, short pamphlets (like those published by Prickly Paradigm Press) provide a unique opportunity to distribute a polemic on a subject about which you are passionate (although this will not take the place of a well-researched book from a prestigious press in your tenure review).

Collaborative productions with those who are the subjects of your research or activists who work on the subject that you have researched can be incredibly gratifying and creative. Such productions might take the form of websites or exhibits of ethnographic information at a university or community museum, photo-essays, videos, or writing projects (such as books aimed at schoolchildren, documents for use in legal proceedings, historical documentaries, or publicity materials). Remember that your students often have amazing technical knowledge for developing websites as well as audio and visual materials and are often eager to apply their knowledge to projects they believe are important and relevant. Again, these do not take the place of peer-reviewed articles and published books in your tenure review, which means you must develop this kind of collaborative work alongside your academic work.

FURTHER READING

One of the best ways to improve one's ethnographic writing and to understand how different writing styles appeal to different audiences is to read a lot. Read ethnographies, but also literary nonfiction and fiction to compare style, form, and structure for how to tell a great tale that delivers the impact you seek. Anthropologists have frequently cited ethnographic writers outside the discipline such as Anne Fadiman, Barbara Ehrenreich, and Philip Gourevitch as authors who offer models of clarity, drama, insight, and empathy about human experience. To this list, I would add Mark Dowie for his *Conservation Refugees*, which demonstrates, for a popular audience, the important insights of anthropology about the conservation practices of indigenous peoples, and William Finnegan, whose works of literary nonfiction, such as *Cold New World*, show him to be one of the best ethnographers of contemporary life around.

10

Linguistic Anthropology

Mary Bucholtz

If you are a linguistic anthropologist, you have the advantage of being able to hold a position in many different sorts of departments, including anthropology, linguistics, area studies, communication, and others besides. But this advantage on the job market also comes with its own challenges once you secure a position. In particular, the publishing expectations of your new department may be quite different from those of the department where you received your Ph.D. training. It is therefore crucial to find out what is expected of you, especially but not only in your first tenure-track job.

You will probably find that this information is surprisingly hard to come by. Very few departments have explicitly stated requirements regarding the type, number, and caliber of publications needed for tenure, and for very good reason: each tenure case is different and must be evaluated on its own merits. At the same time, departments usually have tacit general expectations about how much you should be publishing, in what form, and where your work should appear. Some schools publish the criteria or guidelines that tenure committees use, and these documents can be useful as well. Guides typically cover multiple disciplines, so they do not replace the information you can get from your departmental colleagues and chair. Thus, the most effective strategy for learning about these expectations is to informally raise the question with as many members of your department as you can, from recent hires to newly tenured associate professors to the most senior faculty, and of course your chair. Don't ignore faculty who aren't currently research active; every vote on your tenure case counts equally, and it's helpful to get all perspectives. The responses will no doubt conflict, and it's up to you to decide how to make sense of the information you receive; but you'll begin to get a picture of the factors that will be considered when you're evaluated for tenure.

You can also take an active role in your own tenure case by helping to shape how your publication record is interpreted. Once again, linguistic anthropology has some special advantages and challenges in this regard. Because the field is relatively small and rather technical, it may be a bit mysterious to your colleagues. Sometimes that can work to your benefit: they may be impressed by your expertise. But even so, you will need to educate them—as well as administrators like your chair, the dean, and university-level personnel committees—about the publishing practices in your field. The remarks here will give you some idea of the range of these practices, but you should talk to your advisor, other mentors, and other linguistic anthropologists at different career stages and in different sorts of positions in order to get a clear sense of how publishing works in linguistic anthropology.

The suggestions here are intended to be useful to aspiring academics regardless of department or career stage. Because this book focuses on publishing, my comments are limited to that issue. Keep in mind that there may be significant hiring, tenure, and promotion criteria beyond publications (e.g., teaching or service to the university and discipline) that you should understand and try to meet as well. If you are still on the job market or haven't begun your job search yet, or if you currently have a job but would like to change positions, you should publish with an eye toward the sort of position you'd like to have. A good general goal is to aim to publish one article per year, on average, although the norms for individual departments and for individual faculty may be higher or lower. You should also keep in mind that different disciplines tend to publish at different rates: communication scholars, for example, generally publish much more rapidly than most anthropologists. It's therefore important to make sure you won't be held to norms that don't apply to your own field (although publishing more than others in your department will generally work in your favor).

JOURNALS AND RESEARCH ARTICLES

The gold standard of academic publishing is the *peer-reviewed research article*, that is, a journal article that has undergone anonymous (or "blind") evaluation by one or more specialists in the field. Typically, a manuscript is reviewed by two or three referees who offer different sorts of expertise. Although it is possible to get tenure without a book in some disciplines, in most research universities it is very difficult to get tenure without at least a few journal articles.

Because writing an article for a specific audience is easier than writing without a readership in mind, it's highly advisable to identify a target journal for each of your articles early in the writing process. Choosing a journal involves two different issues: the journal's focus and its status within the field. A typical study in linguistic anthropology could in principle be submitted to many different sorts of journals. You might consider a general anthropology journal; a linguistics journal in sociolinguistics, discourse analysis, or pragmatics; a specialist journal in your geographic area or one that is published in your field language; or a journal focused on the specific topic of your work (e.g., gender, religion, globalization). You will need to decide which of these audiences you primarily want to reach with your article and then frame your work accordingly. But you also need to consider how specific journals may be viewed by your current or ideal future department. In some departments, publications in other disciplines or languages may be frowned upon; in others, they may be warmly welcomed. Generally, a department in which most faculty come from one disciplinary tradition are likely to privilege the elite journals of that discipline. Some departments even have an approved list of journals. In contrast, smaller schools often have multidisciplinary departments (such as a combined sociology/anthropology department). Area studies departments likewise include a spectrum of disciplines and typically are accustomed to reviewing historians, modern language scholars, linguists, archaeologists, political scientists, and so forth according to the standards of those individual disciplines.

It's always safe in the short term to publish within the discipline that currently employs you, but this decision may limit you if you want to change jobs later on. Another possibility is to direct your work to multiple audiences and to publish broadly in anthropology, linguistics, and other relevant fields, a strategy that leaves your career options open but may also diffuse the impact of your work. Some scholars publish similar articles for different audiences to ensure maximal impact. This approach is usually fine if you make the articles clearly different from each other. In any event, you should be aware of which of your colleagues may be on your promotion and tenure committee and make sure that your dossier includes some of the journals with which they are familiar.

The second issue is the prestige of the journal. You should poll advisors and colleagues regarding their views of the relative rank of different journals, but as a rule, a prestigious journal will have at least some of the following attributes: (1) it is the flagship journal of a major professional organization, (2) it is published by a high-profile and well-respected press, (3) it frequently publishes work by top scholars. It is also useful to be aware of citation rankings for journals, such as the impact factor or, more recently, the h-index. Some review committees request that these rankings be listed after each article you publish, a hint that these committees prefer journals with high citation rankings. Within linguistic anthropology, however, there is generally less attention to these concerns because of the tendency for scholars to publish in edited volumes, for which impact factors are not calculated, as well as in journals. A common piece of advice is to submit a manuscript to the best journal first (or the best one that you can reasonably expect might be interested in your work) and then to work down to less prestigious journals if your piece is rejected at the first journal you target. If you have time, this approach can pay off with a high-profile publication. However, you may be anxious to get a publication out quickly, and so you might choose a smaller, newer, or more specialized journal with a reputation for a speedy review process (again, this is something you should ask others about, especially people who have recently published in the journal). As for the question of whether to publish a few articles in top journals or a larger number of articles in respected but less prestigious journals, both strategies have pros and cons, and it's probably best to strive for a middle ground, placing one or two articles as high as you can while publishing several more in good second-tier journals.

Two final matters that are of particular concern to linguistic anthropologists are the publication of an article in a special issue of a journal and the publication of a chapter in an edited volume. Both are common forms of publication in linguistic anthropology, and although they might seem very similar, they are not necessarily treated the same way by those evaluating your research record. A *special issue* is a journal issue comprising a set of thematically linked articles assembled by one or more guest editors, with oversight from the journal's editor. Although individual journals handle the review process for special issues differently, such publications are usually considered equivalent to regular journal articles. An *edited volume* is a book containing chapters by different authors on the same general topic or theme, assembled by one or more scholars who act as the editors of the volume. In some cases a special issue may be expanded into an edited volume. The review process for edited volumes varies widely, and some departments consider book chapters equivalent to journal articles, but others see them as less prestigious. If edited volumes are important publication outlets for you, you should make your colleagues and your dean aware of the status of such volumes in linguistic anthropology.

BOOK-LENGTH WORKS

Junior scholars are often unsure whether they should publish their dissertation in book form or as a series of articles. There is no single answer to this question, since a great deal depends on your department and discipline. Many anthropology departments expect linguistic anthropologists to produce a book before tenure—typically a *monograph*, or specialized research report, based on but different from your dissertation—while many linguistics and communication departments do not, and other fields vary widely. Because linguistic anthropology does not have an established norm, you may be able to negotiate your own requirements with your department. Make sure your chair codifies this understanding in writing, or else you may find yourself in a difficult spot if there's an administrative turnover before your case is decided. When in doubt, it's a good idea to aim for a book along with several articles and book chapters rather than pinning all your hopes on one form of publication or the other. And whatever you decide, start moving your dissertation into published form early! It will take longer than you think.

One challenge currently facing linguistic anthropologists seeking to publish books is that the academic publishing industry is moving away from monographs and toward volumes that can be marketed to a wider audience, such as undergraduate classes or even the general public. Linguistic anthropologists have the additional disadvantage of working with unfamiliar languages and often focusing on technical matters of linguistic structure or the details of discourse. As you develop your book proposal, highlight the ways that you will make your work accessible to a broad audience. This may mean simplifying your writing and analysis a bit or framing the project in relation to big-picture issues rather than focusing exclusively on specialist concerns. In addition, junior scholars may find it increasingly difficult to publish a book without a previous track record of journal articles. It's therefore a good idea to publish a couple of related articles early on to establish your reputation in the area. It can also be useful to publish a version of one chapter in article form, which serves as a kind of advance publicity for the book and helps build your audience.

As noted, edited volumes and special journal issues are a common way for linguistic anthropologists to circulate their work. If you are interested in editing a volume or special issue, think carefully about what it will entail. Writing a proposal, keeping authors on schedule, commenting on their drafts, coordinating the review process, and going over page proofs is a tremendous amount of work, and it will inevitably take time away from your own research. Moreover, the amount of credit you receive for editing work is usually not commensurate with the amount of time you put into it. Nevertheless, it can be worth publishing a special issue or edited volume if you can assemble a cohesive group of researchers doing similar work on a topic of wide interest. Certainly such activities can have a big impact on the field, and so it may be worth pursuing them, especially if you already have the security of a solid publication record. Special issues are usually a bit more manageable than edited volumes because they are typically shorter, and the journal will already have a structure for the review process in place. It's often a good idea to publish a special issue first and then decide based on your experience whether to expand the project into an edited volume.

CONFERENCES

Although it's important to attend conferences in order to stay professionally engaged and receive feedback on your work before you submit it for publication, at research universities conference presentations typically count for very little at tenure time. Certainly, if you're a keynote speaker at a conference or you have been invited to give a colloquium talk in a prestigious department, these activities will be counted as evidence of your stature in the field, but they will not make up for a weak publication record. You should therefore view conferences as the first step in moving your work toward publication rather than as an end in themselves. This means that you should be selective in which conferences you attend, which can be difficult to do in linguistic anthropology because of the large number of potentially relevant conferences. It's much easier to give conference talks than to polish your writing to publishable quality, and it's often tempting to seek out the more immediate rewards of applause and admiring comments than to face the far more critical comments of peer review. But only the latter will make your work excellent. You should choose conferences that represent your key audiences, because your reviewers will likely be drawn from these groups.

Another important role of conferences is to establish professional networks with like-minded peers, often through organizing or participating in thematic sessions or panels. Such panels can be an excellent starting point for a special issue or edited volume; if your panel was well attended and received strong positive feedback, it's a good candidate for publication. Even if you're not primarily interested in editing, it's a good idea to organize one or two panels at AAA early on so that you can begin to make the professional contacts that will provide crucial support for you throughout your career.

MULTIMEDIA PROJECTS

Although linguistic anthropologists have been at the forefront of the use of new technologies for research, the field hasn't yet engaged deeply in alternatives to traditional scholarly outlets. Many departments will give some credit for activities such as documentaries or other video products, research-related websites or blogs, data archives and corpora, software, and so on, although not all of these will necessarily be counted as equivalent to research publications. Once again, educating your department about the value of such work—ideally, by documenting its impact—is essential to getting the credit you deserve. And again, it's safest if nontraditional activities are accompanied by more conventional publications. One effective strategy is to write research articles that focus on your nontraditional work, thus calling greater attention to it as well.

OTHER ISSUES

If you become known for your work in a particular area, you may be invited to write a *survey article* or *chapter* providing an overview of the state of knowledge in that area. Such publications may or may not be peer reviewed in the usual way, but they are usually viewed as prestigious because they are a measure of your stature in the field and they often appear in high-profile review journals or in major reference volumes or handbooks. Not all invited publications in edited volumes are equally prestigious, so consider the topic, the publisher, the editor, and the time it will take you to do the work in making your decision.

A number of linguistic anthropologists occasionally coauthor or coedit publications with colleagues. There are obvious intellectual and practical benefits to doing so, but collaboration is not necessarily an easy route to publication: developing a project with others can be time consuming and can involve a great deal of negotiation and compromise. In addition, such work is weighted differently by different departments and disciplines. Some treat coauthored or coedited publications as equivalent to singly authored or edited work, while others—especially those in which collaboration is unusual—may place less value on these scholarly products. If you want to pursue joint publications, it's a good idea to ensure that these are balanced by a strong record of individual work.

Finally, many linguistic anthropologists are deeply engaged in activities involving activism, outreach, and teaching. These activities and publications about them are welcomed by most departments, although teaching-related publications like textbooks are usually treated as secondary to research-oriented writings about these topics.

As you develop your publication record, resist the urge to compare yourself with anyone else. As mentioned at the outset, everyone's case is different. Bear in mind that you see only others' publication successes, not their rejections or setbacks. In addition, although it's useful to gather as much advice as you can, you should not follow others' publication practices or advice—including the advice in this chapter!—if it doesn't seem right for your situation. Your first concern should be to produce work that you are proud of and to make it available to readers who will be most interested in it. A steady stream of good research, far more than a single splashy book or a mountain of less than journal articles, is the most assured route to a successful academic career.

FURTHER READING

The *Journal of English Linguistics* has a series of editorials on professional matters, including the following pieces on the publication process:

Bucholtz, Mary. "In the Profession: Peer Review in Academic Publishing." *Journal of English Linguistics* 38 (2010): 88–93.

Curzan, Anne, and Robin Queen. "In the Profession: Academic Publication." *Journal of English Linguistics* 34 (2007): 367–372.

Johnstone, Barbara. "In the Profession: Choosing the Right Journal for Your Manuscript." *Journal of English Linguistics* 37 (2009): 1–5.

RESOURCE

Resources for Sociocultural Linguistics
http://www.linguistics.ucsb.edu/faculty/bucholtz/sociocultural

11

Medical Anthropology

Linda M. Whiteford and Cecilia Vindrola Padros

In this chapter, we share some ideas of how to get published in medical anthropology and some lessons learned from the points of view of a current graduate student and a senior professor. The entrance into the academic world as a graduate student is an exciting and intimidating process. Doubts about our ability to contribute something original and innovative to our discipline constantly emerge, and we tend to diminish the value of our own research. The reviews we receive on our work can be both motivating and incredibly disheartening. At first we tend to take things personally and might think we are not cut out for a process in which others can critique our work but we are not allowed to respond to their comments (at least not directly). With time, we get used to the inner working mechanisms of academic publishing and learn to enjoy both positive and negative reviews, as both provide us with information on how to improve our research and writing.

JOURNALS

Research produced within medical anthropology tends to combine multiple areas of inquiry, thus enhancing the already multidisciplinary character of the subfield. Due to the complex issues examined and the fact that most medical anthropologists are concerned with the direct implications of their research, most published research reflects a combination of theoretical frameworks as well as multiple and mixed methodologies directed toward both theoretical and applied purposes. These arrangements produce rich texts that can be published in a wide variety of journals. Table 11.1 lists journals that the Society of Medical Anthropology has compiled and presented on their website. This

Table 11.1. Journals Where Medical Anthropologists Publish

Anthropology	*Medical Anthropology*	*Health and Social Science/ Medical Humanities*	*Public Health/International Health/Global Health*
American Anthropologist	*Anthropology & Medicine*	*Addiction*	*Acta Tropica*
American Ethnologist	*Culture, Medicine and Psychiatry*	*Age and Ageing*	*American Journal of Epidemiology*
Annual Review of Anthropology	*Curare*	*Body and Society*	*American Journal of Public Health*
AnthroGlobe	*Global Change and Human Health*	*Culture, Health and Sexuality*	*Annals of Tropical Medicine and Parasitology*
Anthropoetics	*Journal of Ethnobiology and Ethnomedicine*	*Disability and Society*	*Annals of Tropical Paediatrics*
Anthropological Theory	*Journal of Ethnopharmacology*	*Ethnicity and Health*	*Critical Public Health*
Anthropology Today	*Medical Anthropology*	*Health: An Interdisciplinary Journal for the Social Study of Health, Illness and Medicine*	*Emerging Infectious Diseases*
Cultural Anthropology	*Medical Anthropology Quarterly*	*Health and Human Rights*	*European Journal of Public Health*
Current Anthropology	*Studies in Medical Anthropology*	*Health & Place*	*Global Public Health*
Ethnos: Journal of Anthropology		*Health Education Research*	*Globalization and Health*
Ethos		*Health, Risk and Society*	*Health Education Research*
Field Methods Journal		*Human Ecology*	*Health Policy and Planning*
Human Organization		*Journal of Health Communication*	*International Journal of Environmental Health Research*
Identities: Global Studies in Power and Culture		*Journal of Health, Population and Nutrition*	*International Journal of Epidemiology*
Journal of Gender Studies		*Journal of Health and Social Behavior*	*International Journal for Equity in Health*
Journal of Historical Sociology		*Journal of the History of Medicine and Allied Sciences*	*International Journal of Health Services*
Journal of Political Ecology		*Journal of Social Work Practice*	*Journal of Epidemiology and Community Health*
Journal of the Royal Anthropological Institute		*Psychology, Evolution and Gender*	
Practicing Anthropology		*Qualitative Health Research*	
Public Anthropology			
Science as Culture			
Theory in Anthropology			

Reproductive Health Matters	*Journal of Health Care for the Poor and Underserved*
Social History of Medicine	*Journal of Health Services Research and Policy*
Social Medicine / Medicina Social	*Journal of Public Health*
Social Science & Medicine	*Journal of Public Health Policy*
Sociology of Health and Illness	*Journal of Refugee Studies*
World Health & Population	*Journal of Rural and Remote Health*
	Studies in Family Planning
	Tropical Medicine and International Health

Source: Adapted from the SMA website: http://www.medanthro.net/academic/researchtools.html.

list demonstrates the wide array of publication sources sought by medical anthropologists and the diverse audiences to which they disseminate the results of their research. Authors should consider the fit between what they are writing, the methods and techniques they use, the reputation of the journal within a specific subfield, and the audience they wish to reach before submitting.

Multidisciplinary research has its challenges. One of the difficulties of publishing beyond anthropology journals (e.g., *Medical Anthropology Quarterly*) is addressing the diversity of nonanthropologist reviewers. For an article to be accepted in a nonanthropology journal, the article must transmit the relevance of a medical anthropology perspective and its contributions and must do so without an overreliance on jargon. Jargon, long the mark of successful graduate school experience, can become a barrier that reduces the cross-disciplinary effectiveness of an article. The medical anthropologist attempting to publish in journals directed at other disciplines must keep in mind the nonanthropologist reader and match the topic and overall structure of the article to the journal's policy and audience. To do this effectively, pay close attention to the conventions of the journal to which the article is submitted. Read the articles in a sample issue of the journal in question. Notice, for instance, if they all use a similar structure (objective, method, results, conclusion), or note if they all situate their research problems in the parlance of public health. These clues and the author instructions will guide you in terms of understanding how to frame your paper so that it is most likely to be accepted by the journal.

Publishing, like any other enterprise (for instance, securing a job or preparing for an interview), entails research on the journal content, the editorial board, and its target audience. Students would be well advised to identify the orientation of the journal before submitting an article for review. Here are some questions to ask yourself: Is the journal theoretically oriented? Does it have a particular geographic focus? What kinds of methods appear most often, for instance, mixed methods, statistical, ethnographic, large-scale surveys, life histories, or clinical reviews? When looking at recent back issues, has research like the type you are submitting been published before? What overall structure do these previous articles use? It is also helpful to identify the members of the editorial board and their research interests. Many times when the editorial board changes, so does the focus of the journal. Finally, it can be useful to research the journal's impact factor, its ranking within the subfield of interest, and the method it uses for the review of submitted articles (e.g., if it uses peer review). These last points are important during the process of resume evaluation, when articles published in journals that are highly regarded in the discipline or with a high impact factor might be favored.

One question often asked is whether it is better to submit individual articles to journals or to submit as part of an organized group, such as part of a symposium issue or edited book-length collection. Organized panels for professional meetings such as the American Anthropological Association and Society for Applied Anthropology provide good opportunities for exposure for graduate students, and frequently the panelists or a member of an editorial board or press will suggest that the presentations be published. If this is the case, the student should carefully consider the quality of the other presentations and the commitment of the other panelists to transform their presentations into publishable articles and chapters. Publishing with a group can be very helpful if the papers are good (and perhaps some known authors), but it can also be slow, as not all individuals work at the same pace in completing their work. A single-authored article of high quality may be easier to produce and get through the publication process than a group contribution. On the other hand, being with an innovative or exciting group of articles can bring good attention to the work of an emerging scholar. There are some journals that prefer compiling similar articles into thematic issues, while others are more inclined toward presenting a variety of topics in each issue and will not be keen on publishing a collection of works. In considering the submission of an article as part of a thematic issue, obtain information on who the other authors are and what they have established as their research interests and focus.

BOOK-LENGTH PUBLICATIONS

In addition to the publication of articles in journals, students might have the opportunity of writing a chapter in an edited book or publishing a book (usually based on their dissertation research). Good advice, we think, is to develop the dissertation into a book as soon as you complete the degree and get a job, particularly if it's a job in an anthropology department. However, keep in mind that if you are going to be evaluated by scholars in public health or medicine, you might be better off making sure you have a large number of journal articles, including some in journals that will be readily identified by your review or tenure committee. Your dissertation is a gold mine—it is research completed, vetted, and approved. Use it, whether you polish and refine it into a book-length work or into several journal articles.

CONFERENCES

Annual meetings of professional associations are very useful both for their intellectual as well as social components. All professions have such meetings, whether they are of international educators, informal science providers, water systems managers, or academic anthropologists. Attendance by anthropologists is appropriate at each of these examples, and anthropologists should be encouraged to attend the professional association meetings of their workplace and also of their profession. Many academic medical anthropologists participate in the annual meeting of the Society for Medical Anthropology (SMA); many researchers and students also present papers and posters at the meetings of the American Anthropological Association and the Society for Applied Anthropology. Depending on their research interests, medical anthropologists also participate in other conferences or academic events related to their specific areas of interest. Papers and posters can be presented at meetings focused on specific geographical regions such as the annual meeting of the Latin American Studies Association. Because we believe that it is important for emerging anthropologists to both maintain their intellectual home and develop a broad reach in practice, we have listed below some information adapted from the SMA website on a variety of interest groups where students might meet and contact other researchers working on topics similar to their own.

- Medical Anthropology Students Association: http://www.medanthro.net/research/masa/index.html
- Children and Childhood Interest Group: http://aaacig.usu.edu
- AIDS and Anthropology Research Group: http://groups.creighton.edu/aarg
- Alcohol, Drug, and Tobacco Study Group: http://www2.aptron.com/~adtsg
- Clinically Applied Medical Anthropology: http://www.medanthro.net/research/cama/index.html
- Complementary and Alternative Medicine and Integrative Medicine Group: http://socscicamim.net
- Council on Anthropology and Reproduction: http://sites.google.com/site/anthrorepro
- Council on Nursing and Anthropology: http://www.conaa.net
- Critical Anthropology of Global Health Study Group: http://www.medanthro.net/research/cagh/index.html
- Disability Research Interest Group: http://www.medanthro.net/research/disability/index.html
- Human Sexuality and Anthropology Interest Group: http://hsaig-aaa.ning.com
- Interest Group for the Anthropology of Public Policy: http://aaa-igapp.net
- Science, Technology, and Medicine Group: http://www.medanthro.net/research/stm/index.html

Formal participation in academic meetings (paper or poster presentations) can be highly beneficial for students. Research proposals and reports from as-yet-unpublished theses or dissertations can be presented, and the comments from the audience or other members of the panel can help the student limit the focus of the study or reformulate parts of the data collection and analysis processes. However, another important aspect of participating in conferences that tends to be overlooked is the potential these meetings have for creating contacts with other graduate students and professors. It is beneficial for students to select panels related to their research interests, identify important elements from these presentations, and contact the presenters. The student becomes familiar with the trends in current research produced within his or her area of interest as well as with the experts on these issues. In this way, students connect both with the intense focus of their dissertations and with a wide breadth of related topics. For instance, one might be studying pediatric oncology and find that there is not much published on this topic from a medical anthropology perspective. Attending conferences organized by other disciplines such as nursing or psychology might allow the student to acquire more knowledge on the topic. When establishing conversations with presenters, the student can become aware of the larger issues that are being discussed in terms of the delivery of health services to children, while making themselves (and their research topic) known to other child health specialists.

Another suggestion for graduate students, especially those conducting fieldwork outside the United States, is to participate in conferences and other academic events in the countries where they are conducting their research. This is a useful way of disseminating the results of their research among the local population, but it is also a way of obtaining a different perspective on the study. Useful contacts are made during these meetings with other graduate students and professors who might have practical advice about where to look for information (for instance, libraries or archives that the student was not aware of) and who might also invite the student to participate in other events or publications. The World Council of Anthropological Associations (http://www.wcaanet.org) contains information on anthropological academic associations that group anthropologists from different parts of the world.

WEB-BASED RESOURCES

Medical anthropologists are not limited to the previously mentioned mechanisms of information dissemination. Digital resources are increasingly being used to present the results of research, propose new areas of inquiry, or establish discussions on recent events. There is a robust and ever-growing list of websites created by medical anthropologists that discuss issues of interest to this subfield. The "Resources" section lists some of the blogs that have been active.

Even though blogs are becoming very popular in the field of medical anthropology, it is important to consider that the dissemination of results or ideas through this medium might not receive the same value during the hiring process as articles published in peer-reviewed journals. Furthermore, the anthropologist may not be able to publish results in academic journals that have been previously presented in a blog or other online format. However, many medical anthropologists do not aspire to academic jobs, and blogging can be a useful way of broadcasting your expertise, particularly if your career will be with nongovernmental organizations or hiring firms that do not expect to see a robust dossier of peer-reviewed contributions.

Anthropologists also communicate through different e-mail listservs. In addition to the listservs of each academic department, it is useful to register for the listservs of academic associations or the interest groups presented in the previous section. Through these listservs, you might obtain information on conferences, calls for papers, and new books and journals and hear ideas about teaching or research.

CONCLUSION

In this brief chapter, we have shared our ideas, knowledge, and experience of how graduate students who are interested in medical anthropology may best maximize their time and resources to connect with their larger peer group through professional publications and attendance at professional meetings, making decisions of when, what, and how to publish and with whom. Given the remarkable diversity of the discipline of anthropology and the subdiscipline of medical anthropology, we encourage you to explore the resources provided here as starting points for further research in particular areas of interest.

FURTHER READING

Hewett, Kathryn. "How to Publish Your Journal Paper." *Monitor* 33, no. 8 (2002): 50. http://www.apa.org/monitor/sep02/publish.aspx.

RESOURCES

American Anthropological Association Career Center
http://www.aaanet.org/profdev/index.cfm
Consortium of Practicing and Applied Anthropology Programs "Tenure and Promotion for Applied Anthropologists"
http://www.copaa.info/resources_for_programs/index.htm#tenure
Society for Medical Anthropology List of Resources
http://www.medanthro.net/academic/researchtools.html

Blogs

Access Denied: A Blog about Unauthorized Im/migration and Health
http://accessdeniedblog.wordpress.com
Neuroanthropology
http://blogs.plos.org/neuroanthropology
Somatosphere: Science, Medicine, and Anthropology
http://www.somatosphere.net

Listservs

H-MedAnthro Discussion Network
http://www.h-net.org/~medanthro

12

Visual Anthropology

Peter Biella

This chapter is written primarily to help visual anthropologists publish their textual and visual works, which can assist in the process of getting hired, retained, and promoted within academia. Information about publishing can also help scholars who plan to use anthropology and media in real-world, applied contexts. Other visual anthropologists, whose goals are to be full-time filmmakers or photographers or who wish to work in distribution and film archives, may benefit from the sections of the chapter that concern producing and distributing nonprint media.

Because this is meant as a practical guide, I begin by being practical (see fig. 12.1). Almost every new anthropology job opening in the United States is announced in *Anthropology News*. Between 2007 and 2010, 16 job announcements included the word "visual" (those 16 jobs were announced 29 times). Strikingly, of the 16, only 5 appeared to require the full-time teaching of visual courses. In the other 11, "visual" was mentioned as one possible course option among others. Most announcements sought applicants to teach one or more courses in "visual anthropology," while 3 named "visual culture," 1 "visual arts," and 1 "visual modes of power." During this three-year period, jobs requiring a cultural anthropologist were 14 times more numerous than those specifying "visual."

Figure 12.1 makes it all too clear that the global economic collapse that began in late 2008 correlates with a deep crisis in anthropology and academic hiring. With the realization of this difficult—even grave—situation, two other facts must also be recognized: (1) far more important for a beginning anthropologist than getting published is getting hired, and (2) most important for getting hired are the research subject of one's dissertation and publications. Recently degreed visual anthropologists, like their cultural anthropology

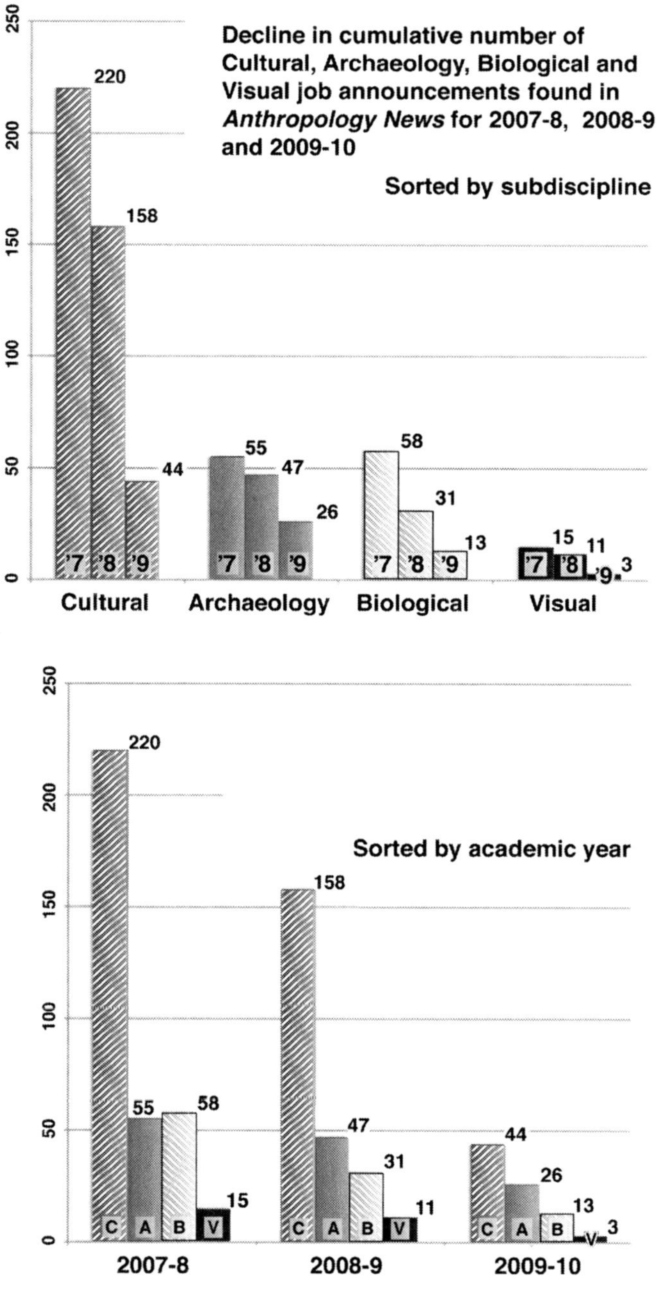

Figure 12.1. Anthropology News *announcements of employment opportunities in subfields of anthropology, 2007–2010. The number of announcements is roughly twice that of actual jobs.*

counterparts, need employment, and the academic jobs are in the cultural subfield. Thus the RUPVA—the Righteous but Utterly Pragmatic Visual Anthropologist—should focus everything, especially the dissertation topic, on getting the interview.

The choice of dissertation topic is the single most important factor influencing one's chance for employment. That choice, buttressed by resulting conference presentations and publications, must be paraded large in vitas, letters of recommendation, and job applications. That choice will make the expert in visuals attractive to the hiring committees that are probably not dominated by visual anthropologists.

The RUPVA must remain true to her vision of visual anthropology and realistic about the job ratios, as seen in figure 12.1. The well-tempered visual anthropologist will be sure to publish some articles that are demanded by culturally focused hiring and promotion committees. Film studies departments are likely to people their review committees with scholars who have publishing expectations of their own. These too must be respected.

Then, when the applicant is short-listed for a job because her work demonstrates the demanded nonvisual expertise, she presents her research before the hiring committee and unveils the magic charm! She reveals that she is not only expert in whatever area of expertise allowed her to stand before the committee in her job talk but is also secretly a dark-glassed, windswept visualist, able to offer classes in that exciting field! Then, only then, will she and her visuals be attractive to the hiring committee. Only then can she assume a proper place in the ranks of the employed.

DRAFTS AND MORE DRAFTS

Visual anthropologists must be versatile and fluent writers, whatever subject they approach. For that reason, much of the following advice about publication is pertinent to cultural anthropologists as well. Neither can escape the importance of rewriting. Thomas Mann understood our problem: "Writers are people for whom writing is more difficult than it is for other people." Soon after I received my Ph.D., I wrote 12 drafts of an essay before I realized what I had to say. Before that point, I had not known how much brain squeezing and groundwork were necessary in normal writing.

Those publishing for the first few times benefit particularly from the advice of peers. Writers' coffee klatches are very useful. Help may also be available from older anthropologists. It is within the rules of the game to telephone a scholar during office hours and ask for feedback on an essay relevant to the scholar's expertise. Some will refuse, but others will understand their professional responsibilities differently and agree to help.

The kindness of strangers is also available to visual anthropologists who would profit from help in film editing. Many filmmakers will be happy to watch a rough cut if the topic reasonably matches their own interests. Assistance in film writing and editing may be found in many ways, including by asking for names from members of the board of directors of the Society for Visual Anthropology (SVA). The words of an expert may make all the difference when moving a film—or an essay—from a draft to a release.

Entering the Gate: Conferences and Journals

First publications seem daunting, but Ph.D. dissertations can be reworked comparatively painlessly and be published either whole or as several independent essays (Anwar 2004; Germano 2005; Luey 2004). An even less painful route to publication is to present dissertation material at conferences. Sessions are occasionally scouted by journal editors, with the papers compiled in a special issue. Sometimes, too, session organizers plan from the beginning to collate all papers into an edited volume.

Whatever the case, visual anthropologists who enter the gates of publication must meet senior scholars and other scholars whose interests coincide with their own. Attendance at annual meetings allows such opportunities. In the United States, the SVA's Visual Research Conference at the annual AAA meeting is particularly important. Because its format is interactive—with question-and-answer sessions interspersed in each presentation—newcomers have many opportunities to recognize sympathetic others and many opportunities to initiate conversation. These talks may lead, by direct or circuitous routes, to funding, distribution, and publication. Another important source of information about colleagues is the SVA section that appears monthly in *Anthropology News*.

If networking is the most agreeable route to publication in a journal, the standard, less agreeable method is to submit articles cold turkey. Journal editors are gatekeepers and bouncers: authors must therefore know the criteria by which editors establish—or dismiss—submissions.

Some editors first jump to an essay's bibliography, as I did when I edited *Visual Anthropology Review*. Sooner or later, however, editors must ask whether an author has something interesting to say. They want articles that open new vistas on the kind of work their journal specializes in publishing. Authors must therefore have a good idea of what issues and approaches the editors of each journal prefer.

Different Journals, Different Foci

Visual writers need to develop familiarity with the variety of topics typically featured in each of the journals related to their field. As producers of the popular 1930s radio broadcast *Zorro* wrote in their guide to scriptwriters, "Do not give Zorro psychological problems. Do not change Zorro's character. People love Zorro just the way he is!" It is easier to find a journal that is sympathetic to one's efforts than to convert a journal to them.

Once, as a student, I submitted to a journal an article in which I sparklingly rebutted an essay written by its recently deceased editor in chief. The ensuing drama forced me to learn the hard way a lesson that I am trying to offer readers here without pain. Prospective authors should identify a journal that is likely to be sympathetic with what they have to say.

Authors should scan recent issues, pay close attention to editorial notes by the current editor, and peruse the information for authors and the aims and scope notes of serials. At the end of this chapter, I list the most visible English-language journals that feature essays in visual anthropology and the URLs with author instructions.

Peer Review

Essays enlighten the world—and they advance one's career. This is especially true when publications appear in journals that are peer reviewed. The vagaries of peer review are discussed at length in Ware (2008). In small-scale publications, this mysterious process begins by drawing reviewers from the journal's advisory board; when outside expertise is required, names may ultimately be drawn from work-flow management systems, which, among other services, provide the names of reviewers sorted by specialization: *American Anthropologist* uses ScholarOne; *Current Anthropology* uses Editorial Manager.

The principle task of peer reviewers is to make recommendations, whether to publish as written, publish with revisions, or reject. Reviewers provide other services as well, not least of which is to give useful feedback to authors whose work they evaluate. As a reviewer, I am most likely to give several pages of criticism if I see hope for a submission with which I am dissatisfied. My reviews mention publications that I think the author should acknowledge, point out weaknesses and strengths in the argument, and query the validity of approaches I think are inappropriate. The following are questions that the editors of *Visual Anthropology Review* request their referees to consider:

- Does the submission have a principal thesis? Is this thesis presented clearly?
- Is the scholarship sound, accurate, well-balanced, and thorough?
- Does the author rely on appropriate sources?
- As a reader interested in this subject, would you consider the submission important enough to recommend to your colleagues? (*Visual Anthropology Review* 2004)

NONPRINT PUBLICATIONS

Creating film, video, photography, and multimedia may be crucial to one's identity and soul force as a visual anthropologist; this output also serves the field. Yet the acknowledgment that nonprint media make a fundamental contribution to the discipline has been long in coming. Twenty-seven years after—and as a distant consequence of—Margaret Mead's (1975) famous dictum that anthropology need not only be a discipline of words, the Executive Board of the American Anthropological Association affirmed the following statement:

> Ethnographic visual media (specifically film, video, photography and digital multimedia) play a significant role in the production and application of anthropological knowledge and form an integral part of the discipline's course offerings. Anthropologists involved in the production of visual works make valuable scholarly contributions to the discipline. . . .
>
> First, the AAA urges [university committees for retention, tenure, and promotion] to evaluate ethnographic visuals as appropriate media for the production and dissemination of anthropological knowledge. Film and video, photography and digital multimedia play increasing roles in research; they are crucial as teaching tools in the discipline's course offerings; and they are often used in applied contexts. (Biella et al. 2002)

These "Guidelines for the Evaluation of Ethnographic Media" have helped advance the careers of many visual anthropologists by assuring faculty members who evaluate their performance that the AAA recognizes visual works as significant professionally. Thus, the RUPVA should not and must not refrain from producing works in film and video, photo-essays, and multimedia, especially after having landed the tenure-track job. Once that barrier is crossed, one's percentage of nonprint publications may be increased.

Film and Video

Film distribution is identified in the AAA guidelines as a legitimate publication venue. When seeking a film distributor, it may be useful to note that the Society for Visual Anthropology's Film, Video and Multimedia Festival has in recent years given the most awards to works distributed by Berkeley Media LLC, Bullfrog Films, Documentary Educational Resources, and Icarus Films. (The "Resources" section of this chapter provides contact information.)

Submission to film distributors begins with a cover letter, a page-long press release, and a DVD. The cover letter should mention whether the film has been included in festivals or won awards before distribution. In some cases, a very short letter of support from a recognized person in the field may be useful, particularly if the film appears to stray from the norm. Only one distributor at a time should be contacted, allowing each the right of refusal before offering the film to another.

Professional distribution is the tried-and-true means to ensure that a film is seen, but not all distributors provide equal service. Some work much harder for the filmmaker than others. The best distributors offer hard-copy mailers, impressive online resources, YouTube clips, and the option of pay-for-view Internet streaming. The filmmaker must check that the distributor's promised efforts are fully itemized in the contract. Since DVDs do not preserve the resolution of contemporary digital media, some additional expenses must eventually be met to provide the distributor with an uncompressed digital version. Self-distribution may bring a filmmaker higher income, since professional distributors keep more than half of the gross on sales and rentals. But distribution includes an enormous amount of mind-numbing work. Moreover, having a recognized distributor is acknowledged to be a professional achievement. (See Garon [2009] for useful information about distribution and the legal and business components of independent filmmaking.)

The inclusion of one's video works in a film festival is also acknowledged by the AAA guidelines to be a publication. Dozens of ethnographic, anthropological, and documentary festivals take place each year. Application forms differ, and the maker is alternately asked to provide 100-, 150-, or 200-word descriptions, often along with an English transcript of the audio track and the film credits verbatim. The most current sources of information about anthropological film festivals are found online (see URLs in "Resources"). Festival attendance allows newcomers a priceless opportunity to meet colleagues who can help them find collaborators, distributors, and funding (Biella 2007: iv).

Just as essays submitted for publication must pass muster with peer reviewers, so too must films be juried to be included in a festival. Like journals, each festival has a characteristic tone and type of subject it favors. All submissions will fare better in some venues than others. To get a sense of the best festival for a film, there is no substitute for attending as many festivals as possible. Unlike the submission of journal articles, one may submit a film to any number of festivals simultaneously. The only limiting factors are application preparation time and festival fees.

Film juries, like that of the SVA Festival which I know best and will describe, have rough and ready, standard criteria for evaluating and selecting films. Anthropological film juries look for a film's grounding in ethnographic fieldwork, its competent engagement with ideas important in anthropology, and its technical proficiency. More than this, juries keep their eyes open for brilliance in nonstandard domains. The SVA has, for example, given one-time awards for "Excellence in Cinematography," "Visual Poetry," and even "Courage under Fire." There is also a "Lost Opportunity" award that is not bestowed because its film designees are not accepted into the festival.

I advise beginning filmmakers to demonstrate all possible excellence in the first three minutes of a submitted film. Jurors must be engaged as viewers from the start, and they cannot always be expected to endure masses of weak material in anticipation that something better will come. Beginning filmmakers usually make their films too long. They must follow the mantra, "When in doubt, cut it out." After they have cut what is doubtful to them, they often need to cut another 20%.

Finally, before filmmakers submit a film to a festival, they should also conduct test screenings with a variety of audiences—not just friends—seeking as much critical feedback as possible. Because a film ultimately must stand on its own, I ask my film production students, when screening their works in class, not to explain the cause of their errors or justify decisions that others do not like. Being quiet helps them listen better. Explanations and unpopular decisions may be described in one's memoirs, but they cut no ice with a critical audience or a film jury.

Whereas writing an essay requires a pencil and paper, writing a video requires a camera, expensive media, and often salaried assistants. These costs add up quickly, and grants are very helpful for completing one's work. To learn the ropes of film grant proposal writing, apprenticeships with successful filmmakers are ideal. Many grant resources can be tracked down through university library subscriptions to databases. I recommend the Foundation Center (http://foundationcenter.org) and GrantStation (http://www.grantstation.com).

Photo-Essays

Although islands of visuality in academia are rising (and the "Guidelines for the Evaluation of Ethnographic Media" constitute part of that slow elevation), the printed word remains academia's privileged medium. Most publications in film theory and the visual arts are print based; many include few visuals. Of the visual publications listed in the "Resources" section, only two have a provision for nonprint submissions!

The journal *Visual Studies* states that it "encourages visually-led submission." Authors and media makers should query the current editor before submitting. In the absence of greater clarification, observation of past publications may best indicate the preferred style. The AAA journal *Visual Anthropology Review* has recently invited photo-essays for peer-reviewed inclusion. Its 2010 editor indicates that the format "consists of a number of photographs with written text directly related to the photos" and suggests that the photos can be within the text or in other configurations. "Whatever the ordering, the images contribute overall a collection of photographs to the essay." And "the author should address in the written text the question of 'Why photography?'" (Buckley n.d.).

Other outlets for visual works abound online: Flikr, for example, is closely watched by interested colleagues as well as by gallery owners looking for material. In addition, the AAA has recently introduced an annual Photo Contest. Winning pictures are digitally projected at the yearly meetings. The SVA offers a periodical John Collier Jr. Award for Still Photography.

Multimedia

The integration of interactive text-based and time-based media is the future of visual anthropology (see Biella 1993, 2009). Since interactivity permits the best available integration of textual scholarship with video, the theoretical with the empirical, it offers the most promising integration of cultural and visual anthropologies. Interactive media is also particularly useful in advancing the analysis of existing films and videos, including those that are ethnographic (Biella, Chagnon, and Seaman 1997). Yet mastering HTML, image making, and one or more subfields of anthropology is very daunting. Perhaps for that reason, and despite the proliferation of web-based instruction, textual scholarship that conducts interactive analysis is still rare. Because this is the discipline's inevitable direction, we must collectively develop peer-reviewed formats for our new work.

Copyright

In much nonprint media production, copyright plays a thorny role. The publication of precopyrighted photographs requires clearance. When visual anthropologists' publications include images from dominant media for the purpose of critique, they (and their editors) must be very clear on the legal labyrinths of copyright and fair use as guaranteed in the First Amendment. One important element of that clarity comes from a 1994 Supreme Court decision that found parody, as cultural critique, to be a permitted form of quotation, despite the copyright holder's objection (*Campbell v. Acuff-Rose Music, Inc.*, 510 U.S. 569). Helpful guidelines on fair use are available from American University's Center for Social Media (Center n.d.; Ad Hoc Committee n.d.), from the International Visual Studies Association (Papademas 2009), and from Stanford University Libraries (SULAIR 2007). For case studies in the perils of jamming the visuals of the powerful, see Lasn (2000), Levin (2003), Westbrook (2006), and Biella (2009: 149).

CONCLUSION

Visual anthropology has always walked a tightrope between artistry and science. The American photographer John Collier Jr. once said that the art of the novel offers the best anthropology. I think he had a point. To show academia the value of our art, we visual anthropologists must take what strength we can from our ineluctably wordy discipline. We need employment; to secure employment, we need to hold our own in publishing. The material base thus assured, we may proceed to visualize in whatever novel medium we choose.

Visual anthropology may strike purists as iffy or not-quite-the-thing. Apart from the fact that most of our visual works have a fleshly foundation in the surface of other people's skin, another cause for skepticism is that we rarely produce our media by ourselves, autonomously. The culture analyst using film or other media has never sallied forth alone, armed solely with notebook and verandah. Our dependence on others has always been manifest: we need someone to do sound, someone else to do picture, perhaps someone to codirect, to help the translations, to watch our back and keep the camera from being stolen. Our dependence on groups and group processes is even more obvious in the case of applied visual anthropology. There, ivory tower doubts about touchy-feely visuals, about popularizers and dirty hands are even more pronounced than they are concerning media makers with no applied intent. Yet visual works have an intimacy that can touch nonacademics and our in-country collaborators more intensely than the most perfectly reasoned essay. Visuals have an irreplaceable role in the global practice—and global understanding—of anthropology. That's why we can't stop and won't stop what we're doing.

FURTHER READING

Ad Hoc Committee on Fair Use and Academic Freedom, International Communication Association. "Clipping Our Own Wings: Copyright and Creativity in Communication Research." Center for Social Media, School of Communication, American University. http://www.centerforsocialmedia.org/fair-use/related-materials/documents/clipping-our-own-wings-copyright-and-creativity-communication-r, accessed April 1, 2011.

American Anthropological Association. "AAA Photo Contest." http://www.aaanet.org/issues/anthronews/photocontest.cfm, accessed August 25, 2011.

Anwar, Mumtaz A. "From Doctoral *Dissertation to Publication*: A Study of 1995 American Graduates in Library and Information Sciences." *Journal of Librarianship and Information Science* 36, no. 4 (2004): 151–157.

Biella, Peter. "Beyond Ethnographic Film: Hypermedia and Scholarship." In *Anthropological Film and Video in the 1990s*, ed. Jack R. Rollwagen, 131–176. Brockport, NY: The Institute, 1993.

Biella, Peter. "Guest Editor's Preface." In "Visual Anthropology of Europe," ed. Peter Biella, special issue, *Visual Anthropology Review* 23, no. 1 (2007): iii–iv. doi:10.1525/var.2007.23.1.iii.

Biella, Peter. "Visual Anthropology in a Time of War." In *Viewpoints: Visual Anthropologists at Work*, ed. Mary Strong and Laena Wilder. Austin: University of Texas Press, 2009.

Biella, Peter, Napoleon A. Chagnon, and Gary Seaman. *Yanomamo Interactive: The Ax Fight*. CD-ROM. Fort Worth: Harcourt Brace, 1997.

Biella, Peter, Jeff Himpele, Kelly Askew, and David MacDougall. "AAA Statement on Ethnographic Visual Media." *American Anthropologist* 104, no. 1 (2002): 303–306. doi:10.1525/aa.2002.104.1.305.

Buckley, Liam M. N.d. "*Visual Anthropology Review* Seeks Photo-Essays." https://listserv.temple.edu/cgi-bin/wa?A3=ind0812e&L=viscom&P=2287&E=1&B=3&T=text%2Fhtml, accessed April 1, 2011.

Center for Social Media. "The Code of Best Practices in Fair Use for Media Literacy Education." Center for Social Media, School of Communication, American University. http://www.centerforsocialmedia.org/fair-use/related-materials/codes/code-best-practices-fair-use-media-literacy-education, accessed April 1, 2011.

Garon, Jon M. *The Independent Filmmaker's Law and Business Guide: Financing, Shooting, and Distributing Independent and Digital Films*. Chicago: Chicago Review Press, 2009.

Germano, William P. *From Dissertation to Book*. Chicago: University of Chicago Press, 2005.

Lasn, Kalle. *Culture Jam: How to Reverse America's Suicidal Consumer Binge—and Why We Must*. New York: Harper Paperbacks, 2000.

Levin, Bob. *The Pirates and the Mouse: Disney's War against the Counterculture*. Seattle, WA: Fantagraphic Books, 2003.

Luey, Beth, ed. *Revising Your Dissertation: Advice from Leading Editors*. Berkeley: University of California Press, 2004.

Mead, Margaret. "Visual Anthropology in a Discipline of Words." In *Principles of Visual Anthropology*, ed. Paul Hockings, 3–10. New York: Mouton de Gruyter, 1975.

Papademas, Diana. "IVSA Code of Research Ethics and Guidelines." *Visual Studies* 24, no. 3 (2009): 250–257.

Society for Visual Anthropology. "Board Members." Effective December 7, 2009. http://societyforvisualanthropology.org/?page_id=32, accessed April 1, 2011.

SULAIR. "Copyright & Fair Use." Stanford University Libraries, 2007. http://fairuse.stanford.edu/Copyright_and_Fair_Use_Overview/chapter9/index.html, accessed April 1, 2011.

Visual Anthropology Review. "Guideline for Referees." 2004.

Ware, Michael. *Peer Review: Benefits, Perceptions and Alternatives*. London: Publishing Research Consortium, 2008. http://www.publishingresearch.net/documents/PRCsummary4Warefinal.pdf.

Westbrook, Steve. "Visual Rhetoric in a Culture of Fear: Impediments to Multimedia Production." *College English* 68, no. 5 (2006): 457–480.

RESOURCES

Journals

Invisible Culture: An Electronic Journal for Visual Culture, published at the University of Rochester
http://www.rochester.edu/in_visible_culture
Journal of *Visual Culture*
http://www.journalofvisualculture.org/submissions
Visual Anthropology
http://www.tandf.co.uk/journals/journal.asp?issn=0894-9468&linktype=44
Visual Anthropology Review
http://www.wiley.com/bw/journal.asp?ref=1058-7187&site=1
Visual Studies
http://www.tandf.co.uk/journals/authors/rvstauth.asp

Anthropological Film Distributors to Investigate First

Berkeley Media LLC
http://www.berkeleymedia.com
Bullfrog Films
http://www.bullfrogfilms.com
Documentary Educational Resources
http://www.der.org
Icarus Films
http://icarusfilms.com

Anthropological Film Festival Announcements

The Newsletter of the Nordic Anthropological Film Association
http://nafa.uib.no
The Society for Visual Anthropology
Annual SVA festival: http://societyforvisualanthropology.org/?page_id=28
Notice of international festivals: http://societyforvisualanthropology.org/?cat=6
Visual Anthropology.net
http://www.visualanthropology.net

Part III

GENERAL DISCUSSIONS

13

Author Agreements

Ricky S. Huard

A contract is an agreement enforceable by law, and the publishing contract is simply a species of this genus. It can be as short as a page or two, or it may run to a dozen or more pages if complex territorial arrangements or options are involved. This chapter will cover only the most basic elements, those common to most, if not all, journal and book publishing agreements. For simplicity, the terms *contract* and *agreement* will be used interchangeably, as will the terms *project* and *work* when referring to the subject matter of the agreement.

The publication of an academic article or book is always a collaborative process, one that involves a certain relationship between author and publisher. The contract lays out the ground rules for that relationship and divides the responsibilities and rewards of the endeavor between the two. A clear understanding of this division at the outset helps ensure fairness and reduces the potential for disagreements later. From this perspective, contract negotiations need not be approached as an adversarial process or a zero-sum game. The common goal, after all, is to produce the best possible article or book and to share it with the largest possible readership.

PRELIMINARY MATTERS

The best advice is quite simple: *read the contract* as soon as it arrives. If there is anything you don't understand or anything you find ambiguous, jot it down and schedule a phone call with your acquiring editor. Publishers are used to fielding these kinds of questions, and it's best to seek clarification sooner rather than later in the publication process. Many book publishers offer an *advance contract* for projects that are still at the proposal or rough draft stage; these agreements are usually contingent on submission of an "acceptable manuscript" by the author or on approval by peer reviewers or an editorial board. Be sure that you understand each contingency on the road to final acceptance by the publisher—missing a deadline or exceeding a page or word count may jeopardize a project. When the final contract arrives, read it carefully as well, making sure it accurately reflects your understanding of the parties' respective rights and responsibilities. Don't assume that it is identical in all particulars to the advance contract.

Always keep a copy of your contract for each project—in fact, keep two. One should stay with the files for the project, and the other should go in a separate file labeled "Publishing Contracts." That way you'll always be able to lay hands on a copy in an exigent moment. You may need to refer to it a few months later, for example, to remind yourself how long you have to review the page proofs. Or you may need to refer to it *years* later, when you want to reuse material from a journal article as part of a monograph or reuse an introduction you wrote in another venue. While your publisher will have the contract on file, publishers do merge or go out of business, and it is much more convenient to have your own copy at hand.

Because of the sheer volume of agreements that they have to deal with, most publishers have standard, one-size-fits-all forms that they use for all works (or for all works of a given type, e.g., one for monographs and another for edited collections). Many contracts, therefore, include a number of boilerplate provisions that may or may not apply to your specific project. Publishers like the convenience of uniformity and generally will want to make as few changes as possible to their standard form. That said, there may be mistakes or small incongruities in your agreement. For example, if your contract contains a clause that says "except as provided in paragraph six" and there *is* no paragraph six, point this out and get it corrected. Your publisher may even thank you. And although many terms are standardized, there are points where you may have some room to negotiate, as I will suggest here.

CONTRACT BASICS

A contract must clearly identify the *parties* to the agreement—usually the author or editor of the work on one side and the publisher on the other—as well as the *subject matter* of the agreement. A working title or description of the project usually is sufficient. For book-length works, there are also such matters as delivery date, length of manuscript, and number and type of illustrations. Each of these points is important, because together they help the publisher determine the cost of producing the work, which in turn must be balanced against the work's price. A manuscript that comes in 20,000 words over limit and with 30 photos instead of 6 line drawings may cost substantially more to produce and thus turn the project from a profitable proposition into a money loser.

In this part of book contracts, you may also encounter the stock phrase, "Time is of the essence." Most publishers are aware that academics, especially young academics, are under severe time constraints—teaching, service, research, and so on—and understand that deadlines sometimes slip. At the same time, too many delays can result in a project's getting off schedule and even being canceled. So be realistic in setting a timetable. It can be easy in the first flush of enthusiasm to agree to an ambitious schedule, either to please the publisher or to see your own work in print. It's better to set a realistic schedule that you can stick to than to set an ambitious one that you'll have to revise at each stage of the publication process. If the contract says that time is of the essence, take this as a sign that the publisher is very serious about deadlines and may be inclined to declare you in breach of contract for more than minimal delays.

For journal articles or shorter contributions, the contract is more likely to be presented after text is in hand and the article has been accepted for publication, so these agreements may not stipulate length. Otherwise, however, the basic terms resemble those for books.

Regardless of whether it's a book or an article under contract, publishing should offer a service to you. This may be given access to a suite of services—peer review, copyediting, typesetting and design, printing, and, most important, distribution—that would be cumbersome for individuals to assemble on their own. Under most contracts, the publisher is responsible for copyediting, typesetting, printing, and (usually) proofreading, although many also allow or require authors to review the copyedited manuscript or the proofs. In book-length works, the author is usually responsible for indexing.

This exchange of the author's original work for the publisher's services forms part of the *consideration*—that is, the quid pro quo—that lies at the heart of the author-publisher relationship. But there is also a less tangible exchange going on here, an exchange of rights. In order for most publishers to incur the costs of copyediting and layout, online or print publication, marketing, and visibility efforts, they will need you to provide them with explicit rights to the work.

COPYRIGHT

The Copyright Act of 1976 (17 USC, sections 101 et seq.) breaks down the author's *copyright* into six basic rights: (1) to reproduce the work; (2) to prepare derivative works from it; (3) to distribute copies of the work by sale or other transfer; (4) to perform the work publicly; (5) to display the work publicly; and, in the case of sound recordings, (6) to perform the work publicly via digital audio transmission. As the author of an original work, these rights vest initially in you, even if you do not register the work with the U.S. Copyright Office or take any other action, unless your writing is a commissioned work or a work made for hire. Any subsequent *transfer* of those rights, generally speaking, must be in writing and signed, with a few exceptions (see 17 USC, Section 201[d]). These rights are entirely *severable*, so you could grant to a publisher the reproduction and distribution rights to a work while retaining the derivative works, performance, and display rights. Each of these rights may be transferred or licensed *exclusively* or *nonexclusively* and with geographic or temporal restrictions. (If you want more information on copyright, you may wish to refer to chapter 14.)

While in theory the six severable rights could be handled with six different agreements, in reality, most publishers will expect you to assign the entire copyright through an *all-rights* clause. As for the name in which the eventual copyright registration is made, this isn't much of an issue in academic publishing. Since you'll be asked to hand over the full rights to the work in most cases, having your name on the copyright page doesn't gain you anything and may actually create confusion in the future (for example, whether to contact the author or the publisher for permission to reprint or excerpt).

Most book contracts contain some form of *reversion clause*, which returns all rights to the author if the publisher allows the work to go "out of print" or fails to make it "available" for a certain period of time. But as short-run digital printing and print-on-demand have become mainstream practices, when and if a book goes "out of print" has become a point of contention. And as long as an e-book file resides on a server somewhere, ready to be downloaded, does it ever become "unavailable"? Instead of relying on these vague locutions, it's better to define a clear trigger event for the reversion of rights to your work. Two common triggers are the failure to meet a minimum dollar sales figure or minimum unit sales figure for a certain period of time. Whether a book has fallen "out of print" or become "unavailable" is a matter of interpretation, but whether the work has sold fewer than 100 units in the last calendar year or has generated less than $1,000 in gross sales for the last reporting period are indisputable facts—and all the evidence you need is on the royalty statement sent to you by the publisher. Reversion of rights is not necessarily automatic upon the occurrence of the triggering event; many contracts require the author to request reversion in writing and may give the publisher an opportunity to reprint within a specific period (six months or a year) before being required to sign over the rights. Does the contract grant you the right to receive a copy of the final files upon reversion of rights? If not, you should ask to include it. This can be a real time-saver if you plan to do other things with the work, such as self-publishing an e-book or a print-on-demand edition.

Most journal publisher agreements require the full copyright in order to support their sales packages, which often include print and online access and often allow course-pack use, distribution in many countries, and so on. So while you may be happy to add that peer-reviewed article or conference paper to your resume, think ahead as you read the journal-publishing contract. Do you plan to use this material again? In what format? What rights do you retain? If later you do find yourself in a contractual bind—you've retained no rights, and the publisher either refuses permission to reprint the article or charges so steep a price as to make it impracticable—don't despair. You can always rewrite the material: copyright attaches only to the expression of the idea, not to the idea itself.

WARRANTIES AND THIRD-PARTY PERMISSIONS

Most publishers will require you to warrant that all material (unless otherwise noted) is original to you and may be copyrighted and that you will indemnify and hold the publisher harmless for any damages for infringement of copyright. This is a CYA clause for the publisher, which doesn't want to get hit with a civil suit or criminal penalty for publishing infringing material that you—wittingly or unwittingly—supplied but did not author. This clause is usually nonnegotiable. However, if you wrote the work in question, there is no doubt you own copyright to it. There is usually a warranty that the work contains no material that is slanderous or libelous or that violates the right of privacy or right of publicity of any person. I've always suspected that these clauses serve a monitory function rather than a practical one. After all, if a publisher is successfully sued by an aggrieved rights holder, the likelihood of that publisher collecting a large indemnity from an impecunious academic seems doubtful, and it is an unlikely publisher who would like to make the news headlines for persecuting an author.

Just as you must warrant the originality of your work, you will also be obligated to obtain—and to pay for—permission to reproduce any third-party material that you incorporate into your work (e.g., photographs, illustrations, or extended quotations not covered by the doctrine of fair use, which is described in chapter 14). Be sure to obtain all the rights that your publisher requests (e.g., print and/or digital, all territories, all languages). Often the publisher will have a sample letter or form for you to use in requesting third-party permissions. If the permissions fees are too steep, remember that you are always free to adapt the information yourself: redraw a map, or cite the data and replot a bar graph into a pie chart. Copyright applies to original works, not to underlying facts, data, or concepts.

ADVANCES AND ROYALTIES

This section applies to books, as journals with their multitude of authors do not offer payment to contributors of articles. Generally speaking, scholarly works are not big moneymakers. The occasional breakout title enjoys popular and financial success, but this is the exception. Most academic journals have a limited readership, and most university press books sell modestly. Because of this, publishers are usually reluctant to pay a large *advance*—that is, a nonreturnable payment to the author against future royalties—for scholarly works. In fact, any advance at all, except for a big-name author with a proven track record, is a rarity.

More usual are *royalties*, periodic payments based on sales of your book, usually expressed as a percentage. Royalty rates may be based on the *list price* of the book or on the publisher's *net* of each sale. Make sure that you understand which standard is used to define your rate. As book sales have languished in recent years, so too have royalty rates. Some publishers have eliminated royalty payments from their standard contracts altogether; others have set high minimum sales targets that must be met before a royalty is paid. I often tell authors who feel slighted by the skimpy royalty rates offered by academic publishers that they're going to make more money from the tenure and promotion value of their book than they ever will from the royalties.

You can try to negotiate a higher rate, but you probably won't make much headway. You're more likely to make progress by negotiating *around* that basic rate, for example, by asking for an *escalator clause*. That is, you'll accept the lower rate proposed by the publisher for the first, say, 500 copies sold, if they'll give you a higher rate for the next 2,000 copies sold, and an even higher rate for the next 5,000. If the publisher anticipates modest sales for your book and is correct in that assumption, the escalator clause costs the publisher nothing. If your book takes off, though, the escalator clause allows you to share in the success of your work. Similarly, if the publisher won't budge on the rate for the hardcover, try negotiating a higher rate for a paperback edition or—and this can be key—any e-book edition. Again, if the publisher is correct in forecasting modest sales, this concession costs nothing; but if reader demand justifies a paperback or digital version, you capture a modest gain.

Income from sales of *subsidiary rights* (e.g., translation, film adaptation, course-pack reprints, electronic reserves) for books is usually split fifty-fifty between the publisher and the author.

OPEN ACCESS AND CREATIVE COMMONS LICENSING

With the growth of the Internet, more universities, libraries, and other entities have established policies on open access (OA) and institutional repositories (IRs). "Open access" is a policy of allowing free access online to read, copy, and distribute copyrighted works, usually for research or scholarly purposes. For example, the Committee on Institutional Cooperation has promulgated on behalf of its member universities an OA policy that includes an addendum for faculty authors to attach to all publishing contracts. The addendum provides that after a period of six months from publication, the author shall have the right to make "the final published version of the work available in digital form over the Internet." Certain grant funders have instituted their own OA policies. The National Institutes of Health, for example, require investigators who receive taxpayer funding through that agency to deposit the final, peer-reviewed versions of manuscripts in the PubMed database for free public access within 12 months of publication. Publishers are understandably loath to allow free access to the very product that they are spending a fair amount of time and money to copyedit, typeset, print, and otherwise develop.

So read your publisher's contract *and* read your home institution's or grant funder's policy on OA. You don't want to get caught in conflicting contractual obligations. If your home institution has an OA or IR policy, examine it carefully to determine which version of the project it requires you to post. Many publishers—journals and book publishers alike—have no objection to your posting the *prepublication* version of the work, that is, the version before peer review. But if the policy requires submission of the actual published version—the version to which the publisher holds the copyright and from which it hopes to make back its investment—you may have to request a waiver from your home institution (all have a policy for how to do this) or to consider placing your manuscript with publishers who will honor such addenda or whose agreements already support deposit mandates.

Creative Commons (CC) offers a licensing scheme that is mostly compatible with OA principles. Wikipedia and the Public Library of Science, for example, operate under CC licenses, which come in four basic types: attribution, no derivative works, noncommercial, and share alike. *Attribution* means that you allow others freely to copy, distribute, display, or perform your work or to create derivative works from it as long as they give you credit for the original material. *No derivative* works means that others may copy, distribute, display, or perform your work verbatim but may not create derivative works. *Share alike* means that others may create derivative works only if they distribute them under an identical license (e.g., attribution or share alike). *Noncommercial* means that others may create derivative works only for noncommercial purposes. If your work incorporates a significant amount of CC-licensed material, particularly if it is under the noncommercial license, your publisher may require you to seek formal copyright permission or to rewrite the material. Be sure to make your publisher aware of this potential conflict so that the material can be evaluated and perhaps worked around.

If you elect to self-publish, whether digitally or in print, a CC license can be a good way of circulating your work more widely than a traditional publishing agreement might, while still retaining some level of control. But if you later take your work to a traditional publisher, the existence of the CC-licensed version may make it harder for the publisher to invest in your work and thus may make it difficult for you to strike a deal.

CONCLUSION

There are many more elements to a typical publishing contract, but you now have an understanding of the basics. When both sides of the contract negotiation have similar expectations and speak the same language, the result is more likely to be a smooth transaction and an agreement that is reasonable and fair to all. Publishers, indeed, often appreciate a knowledgeable author. More complex arrangements may require the assistance of an agent or an attorney, of course, but you now have the ability to represent yourself with a confidence born of knowledge.

FURTHER READING

Creative Commons. "About Licenses." N.d. http://creativecommons.org/about/licenses, accessed April 1, 2011.

Germano, William. *Getting It Published: A Guide for Scholars and Anyone Else Serious about Serious Books*. Chicago: University of Chicago Press, 2001.

Kaufman, Roy S. *Publishing Forms and Contracts*. New York: Oxford University Press, 2008.

Lindsey, Marc. *Copyright Law on Campus*. Pullman: Washington State University Press, 2003.

Owen, Lynette. *Selling Rights*. 6th edition. New York: Routledge, 2010.

Suber, Peter. "Open Access Overview." Last revised November 10, 2010. http://www.earlham.edu/~peters/fos/overview.htm, accessed April 1, 2011.

U.S. Department of Health and Human Services, National Institutes of Health. "NIH Public Access Policy Details." http://publicaccess.nih.gov, accessed April 1, 2011.

14

Copyright

Peter Givler

This chapter discusses the fundamental principles of copyright, how they affect publishing in general and scholarly publishing in particular, and the choices they present as you decide how best to disseminate your own scholarship. Digital technologies have changed the way scholarship is communicated and have opened up choices for you, the author, that didn't exist in a world bound to ink on paper. At the same time, some things about scholarly communication have not changed, or have changed very little. It's important to understand both.

COPYRIGHT AS A LEGAL CONSTRUCTION

First, the basic principles. U.S. copyright law is rooted in Article 1, Section 8, of the Constitution, which enumerates the powers of Congress: to coin money, establish a postal system, create federal courts subordinate to the Supreme Court, declare war, raise and support an Army and Navy, and so forth.

Among those powers, Section 8 stipulates that Congress can "promote the Progress of Science by securing to Authors for limited Times the exclusive right to their respective Writings." (For simplicity I have elided the language referring to patent law, which is also included in this section.) Keep in mind that science in 18th-century usage simply meant knowledge in general. Copyright, then, promotes the advancement of knowledge by granting authors an exclusive but limited private right to what they have written. That right is known in law as one of three types of intellectual property right. Because this is a book for anthropologists about publishing, this chapter focuses on copyright and ignores completely the subjects of patents and trademarks, two other important intellectual property rights.

The limitations on copyright will be discussed further later, but the most important of them deserves mention here. Copyright is of limited duration. Any work not protected by copyright is said to be in the public domain, and public domain works can be freely used by anyone. All works published in the United States before 1923 are in the public domain, as are all works written by U.S. government officers and employees as part of their official duties. Some other works published after 1923 may also be in the public domain; for a full discussion, see Hirtle (2011) under "Further Reading."

The entire copyright statute, 350 pages long in the spring of 2011, is an elaboration of that basic constitutional principle. The length and complexity of the statute derive partly from the fact that, in law, the "works of authorship" to which copyright applies include not just literary works or works intended to be read, but also plays, films, musical compositions, audiovisual works, pantomimes, choreographed works, paintings, photographs, sculptures, and architectural works. Specifying how the law should apply to this variety of expressive forms, each with its own unique characteristics, and taking account of technological advances, is a complex job.

However, the vast majority of scholarly communication today still takes place by means of what the law terms "literary works." Under U.S. law, Title 17 USC, Section 102(a), "Copyright protection subsists, in accordance with this title, in original works of authorship fixed in any tangible medium of expression, now known or later developed, from which they can be perceived, reproduced, or otherwise communicated, either directly or with the aid of a machine or device." In plain English, the law grants you, the author, a copyright in your work. Copyright comes into existence the moment you begin to write, whether in pencil on a sheet of paper or any other "tangible medium of expression," including a computer. Formal registration of the copyright with the U.S. Copyright Office is not required; however, creating a clear public record of copyright ownership through registration with the U.S. Copyright Office does convey certain important benefits, such as the ability to seek statutory damages in a suit for infringement.

The sole requirement for a legal grant of copyright is that the work be "original," a word not defined in the statute but whose legal meaning has been established through court decisions. In the widely cited case of *Feist v. Rural Telephone Company*, the court held that the white pages of a telephone directory did not qualify for copyright protection because simply alphabetizing a list of names and addresses did not produce an original work, but the yellow pages did because they included ads of varying content, typography, shapes, and sizes. As a scholar, you may assume that anything you write in your own words will meet the test of originality under copyright law. However, the academic standards by which scholarly work is judged to be original are quite different. Those standards require that the work of others incorporated into your work, whether by direct quotation or by summary in your own language, be formally acknowledged.

The legal test of originality brings us to the second fundamental principle of copyright law: copyright applies to forms of expression, in the case of academic writing, to the specific choice and arrangement of words on the page. It does not apply to the ideas those words are intended to convey, or to the clichéd elements of a work that necessarily follow from those ideas. Similarly, because facts and discoveries are not, in this legal sense, "original" to the author, there is no copyright protection in them, except for a narrow copyright in their selection and arrangement. In the language of Title 17 USC, Section 102(b), "In no case does copyright protection for an original work of authorship extend to any idea, procedure, process, system, method of operation, concept, principle, or discovery, regardless of the form in which it is described, explained, illustrated, or embodied in such work."

People sometimes assume that a copyrighted work locks up the ideas it contains so they can't be used by others. Nothing could be farther from the truth. The core purpose of copyright is to encourage the communication of new ideas and the spread of new knowledge. It does so by granting a legal privilege to the socially vital work authors do in striving to fix what they have thought in writing so that it can be shared, and further built on, by others. Copyright assumes that nothing grows in a vacuum, that facts are free for all to use, and that new ideas build on the matrix of what has gone before.

A copyright itself consists of six specific rights. For written scholarly work, the first three are the most applicable: the right to make copies of the work, to distribute those copies, and to prepare derivative works (like a new edition or a film based on the work). The other three rights apply to audio and visual works: the right to perform the work publicly, to display the work publicly, and, in the case of sound recordings, the right to perform the work by means of digital audio transmission.

Although the rights to make copies, distribute them, and prepare derivative works clearly would apply to all written scholarly works, and the rights of performance, display, and digital audio transmission only to those written works intended or adapted for other media—film and video, television, the stage, computer display, and so forth—all six rights are granted to you as the author.

These rights are separable. You can, in principle, enter into an agreement about the disposition of some of these rights and retain others, or enter into separate agreements for each of them. You can also choose to exercise some or all of these rights yourself. You can even choose neither to exercise any of them nor to allow anyone else to do so, effectively guaranteeing that the work will be known only by those to whom you show it. But to fully understand the choices you have for exercising your copyright rights, it will be useful to look at the general relationship between copyright and publishing.

COPYRIGHT AND PUBLISHING

The word *publish* stems from a Latin verb meaning "to make public." Because scholarly inquiry is so intellectually and methodologically rigorous, the process of publishing scholarship is particularly refined. It begins with the initial screening of manuscripts. It includes the selection of knowledgeable scholars to write reviews, the evaluation of those reviews and overseeing any revision made in response to criticisms or suggestions for improvement. It includes editing to bring the manuscript's written style into conformity with the scholarly conventions of the academic discipline to which it contributes and the standards of English spelling, punctuation, and usage. It includes the checking of artwork: photographs, charts, graphs, and other illustrative material, which today may include sound files and video clips. It includes design and page layout, and the preparation of electronic files for both printing and screen display. It includes promotion and advertising so that people know the work is available. And it includes systems for delivering the work, possibly as a print artifact or electronic file, to the people who want it.

All of these publishing services require the skills of trained professionals: people knowledgeable about acquisitions, manuscript editing, journals and subscription management, page design, production management, information technology, and order fulfillment. Traditionally, publishers have invested the cash required to pay these people for their services on the expectation that they could recover that investment from subscriptions to and advertising in journals, and sales of books. Part of the economic rationale was the expectation that, as long as the work was legally protected by copyright, publishers would enjoy the exclusive right to publish the work. They would not, in other words, find themselves in the economically untenable position of making a publishing investment only to find that the market from which they had intended to recover their costs had been usurped by others free riding on that investment. Sometimes that free riding is inadvertent, but deliberate copyright piracy has always been a concern, and the explosion of digital publishing has only compounded the problem.

The copyright in your work is granted to you as the author. A publishing contract is the legal instrument through which you and the publisher stipulate the terms under which your work will be published. Chapter 13 deals with author agreements; I will only point out here that the basic "deal" in any such agreement is that the publisher agrees to publish your work provided certain conditions are met, and you agree to assign to the publisher the particular configuration of your copyright rights the publisher needs in order to recover the investment and continue to invest in the publication of new work.

Whatever the publisher's business model may be—and the number and variety of them is wider today that ever before—it's important to remember that publishing has costs, and the money to pay these expenses has to come from somewhere. The copyright granted to you as an author may seem abstract, but it has real value to you as well. That is obvious if you write a successful textbook, or a book that has a wide general audience or that is adapted for film or television. It may be less obvious but it is still true if your work is only published in specialized scholarly journals; copyright provides the legal basis for you to claim authorship of your own work. The reward system in the life of a scholar—promotion, tenure, professional reputation, and advancement—depends heavily on the validity of such claims.

PERMISSIONS, TEACHING, AND SCHOLARSHIP

That the rights granted under copyright are exclusive means that any reuse of a copyrighted work, whether of the entire work or portions of it, requires the permission of the copyright owner or licensee. This principle applies both to the inclusion of someone else's copyrighted work in a work you intend to publish, and to others' copyrighted work you would like to provide to your students in a course you are teaching, whether it be by posting the work on your own website, making it available through a course management system or library e-reserves, or printing out copies to distribute in class. A limited exception to this principle, fair use, is discussed later.

Traditionally clearing permission meant applying directly to the publisher of the work you wanted to use, but today there are an increasing number of licensing arrangements for colleges and universities that can simplify this task. Under these licenses, permissions for reuse of material in the publications covered by the license have been precleared, so no additional permission is necessary. Your library can tell you whether the material you want to use is covered by such an arrangement.

The Copyright Clearance Center (CCC) has entered into agreements with many publishers under which they are authorized to grant permissions on the publishers' behalf. In many cases the process can be completed online (http://www.copyright.com/search.do?operation=show&page=ppu).

If the material you want to use is covered neither by your institution's site licenses nor by the CCC, then you should apply to the publisher directly.

More and more publishers also offer the capability of applying online. You can find permissions guidelines and other useful information, including sample forms and an index of publishers' permissions contacts, on both the Association of American University Presses website and the Association of American Publishers' website (see "Resources").

As long as the publisher holds the requested rights (it may not for third-party material, like artwork), permission to use reasonably short amounts of copyrighted material will almost always be granted for scholarly and teaching purposes, so seeking permission rarely presents an obstacle to use. It can be a speed bump, though. For older works especially, the terms of the contract may need to be checked manually, and in the weeks before the start of a new semester the publisher may be flooded with such requests. In general, you should submit your requests at least a month before the start of classes.

Fair Use

There are various exceptions to the exclusive right of copyright owners stipulated in Title 17, Section 106, but for scholars and teachers, the most important is Section 107, fair use. In the language of the statute, "the fair use of a copyrighted work, including such use by reproduction in copies or phonorecords or by any other means specified by that section, for purposes such as criticism, comment, news reporting, teaching (including multiple copies for classroom use), scholarship, or research, is not an infringement of copyright" (Title 17, USC, Section 107). The statute goes on to stipulate the criteria used to determine whether a particular use of a copyrighted work is a fair use: the "four factors." Before going into the factors, though, it will be helpful to understand a little about the origins of fair use as a concept.

Fair use has its roots in the British common-law notion of "fair dealing," basically the idea that the interests of fairness dictate that judges have the authority to find that although a law has been violated, the violation is permissible under certain circumstances. Here's a simple example. A hungry man is walking past a farmer's orchard, picks up an apple that has fallen on the ground, and eats it. The farmer complains to a nearby policeman, who arrests the man for stealing. The judge, after hearing the facts, rules that although the man did steal an apple, the theft could be allowed because a desirable social result had been achieved—a hungry man had been fed—and because there had been no harm to the interests of the farmer—windfalls would not be part of the farmer's harvest but would be left on the ground to rot. Neither of these two factors—a social benefit achieved and no harm done—considered separately would be sufficient to excuse the theft, but taken together they may under the principle of fair dealing.

Fair dealing has a long history in British common law. Properly applied, it gives judges a flexibility they would not have if they were to strictly apply the king's, or statutory, law. A U.S. version known as fair use was codified in federal law with the Copyright Act of 1976.

Although there are differences between fair use and fair dealing, there are two key similarities. First, their purpose is to provide courts with the flexibility to consider individual circumstances, and therefore their determination is highly fact specific. Second, they are defenses against a charge that a law has been broken; under current law, there is no affirmative right of fair use, because fair use is a legal defense against a charge of infringement.

Essentially, Section 107 outlines four factors to determine whether a particular use of a copyrighted work is a fair use. These are as follows:

1. The purpose and character of the use, including whether such use is of a commercial nature or is for nonprofit educational purposes
2. The nature of the copyrighted work
3. The amount and substantiality of the portion used in relation to the copyrighted work as a whole
4. The effect of the use upon the potential market for, or value of, the copyrighted work.

The important thing to remember is that no single factor is determinative, including whether or not the use is for nonprofit educational purposes. In reaching a determination about fair use, courts have evaluated the use under each of the four factors to decide whether each factor weighs for or against a finding of fair use, and then have made an overall judgment whether the use itself is fair.

Since there are four factors, this process raises the logical question of what a court will do when it finds the factors split, two weighing in favor of fair use and two against. The court must sort it out, but historically judges have given greatest weight to the fourth factor, harm to the market for the work, although some recent decisions have focused on the first factor, specifically on whether the use is "transformative" and alters the meaning of the original. There are some detailed examinations on this complex question in the "Further Reading" section. The lack of clear boundaries about what is and isn't fair use may seem troubling, but think of it as the consequence of a trade-off between flexibility and rigidity, spanning a wide expanse of creative works in varying media and genres.

So when do you need permission from the copyright holder to use portions of a copyrighted work, and when can you rely on fair use? For publishing your own scholarship, the answer is pretty straightforward: your publisher will advise you, based on their knowledge and experience. For teaching—reproducing material to hand out in class, or posting it on your own website, a course management system, or library e-reserves—your college or university should have a clear policy for course use of copyrighted materials and should be able to assist you in particular cases.

If your institution doesn't provide this kind of support and you are left to figure it out on your own, the resources listed at the end of this chapter may help. Nobody expects you to become a lawyer, but if you are going to use the fair use exception, then it is reasonable to expect you to make a good-faith effort to understand its purpose and how it may apply. Its purpose, in your case, is to provide a way of judging the relative weight to be given to the public interests served by scholarship and teaching on the one hand, and the private interests of copyright holders on the other, always keeping in mind that the fundamental purpose of copyright is to promote the growth of new knowledge, and one of the ways it does so is by encouraging investment in the dissemination of existing knowledge.

Finding the right balance is crucial. Some limited exceptions to copyright are consistent with that overarching goal, but if applied too broadly they undermine the incentive for authors to create and publishers to invest and thereby weaken the entire system of scholarly communication. In deciding how to place your own work and the use you would like to make of others' work, remember that for scholarly information, the vast majority of the publishers making that investment are small specialized commercial publishers, nonprofit scholarly societies, and university presses.

FURTHER READING

This chapter references specific provisions of U.S. copyright law but does not go deeply into its technical details. You may wish to refer to any number of excellent books that do, a small selection of which I mention here, or to refer to the U.S. Copyright Office or the statute itself, Title 17 of the United States Code.

If you need personal advice about how the general principles of the law apply to the specific facts of your own work, or to a use you would like to make of someone else's work in your teaching or scholarly writing, you should seek qualified legal counsel.

Gorman, Robert A. *Copyright Cases and Materials.* 7th edition. New York: Foundation Press, 2006.

Hirtle, Peter B. "Copyright Term and the Public Domain in the United States, 1 January 2011." Last updated January 3, 2011. http://copyright.cornell.edu/resources/publicdomain.cfm.

Steven, Daniel. "Do You Need Permission?" 2003. http://www.publishlawyer.com/carousel11.htm.

Wilson, Lee. *Fair Use, Free Use, and Use by Permission: How to Handle Copyright in All Media*. New York: Allworth Press, 2005.

RESOURCES

Association of American Publishers
http://publishers.org/main/Copyright/copyPermission_01.htm?id=20
Association of American University Presses
http://www.aaupnet.org/aboutup/issues/copyright/index.html
U.S. copyright statute
http://www.copyright.gov/title17

15

Collaboration

Don Brenneis

Collaboration lies at the heart of anthropological research in many ways. Certainly in both biological anthropology and archaeology, much research depends on fairly large-scale cooperative work, whether on a site (and in the associated preparation and subsequent analysis) or in the laboratory. Medical anthropologists and practicing anthropologists are also often embedded in larger working groups that may well cut across disciplinary boundaries and move beyond academia. And, for linguistic and cultural anthropologists, the intimate, intersubjective ethnographic encounter is a recurring and inherently collaborative hallmark of field research.

At the same time, the degree and character of collaborative publications vary widely across the discipline as a whole. A far-from-scientific examination of the table of contents of recent issues of major subdisciplinary journals, for example, shows hardly any coauthored articles in cultural or linguistic anthropology. In medical anthropology and human ecology, multiply authored pieces are much more common, and they represent more or less the norm in archaeology and biological anthropology. In archaeology and biological anthropology, single-authored pieces are often either short comments, major theoretical overviews, or bibliographic essays; most "research" publications are collaborative.

So, in thinking about publishing collaborative work, recognizing subdisciplinary variation is important. In some areas collaboration in publication clearly comes with the territory, bearing a close relationship to complex multiparty research practices characteristic of the field and often the subject of explicit training and socialization. In other fields, and especially in linguistic and cultural anthropology, collaborative publication remains much less common, the exception rather than the assumed. Even in those times in the past when fairly large-scale collaborative and comparative research projects were more frequent in cultural anthropology, publications tended to be individually authored. Whether multiple authorship is typical or an outlier doesn't mean that it is or isn't a good idea or an appropriate and generative strategy to pursue. It does suggest, however, that thinking anthropologically, in this instance paying attention to local norms and practices, is a good starting place. Once you consider what conventional practice in your area is, then ask yourself if there are good reasons to write somewhat against the grain. There may well be!

In this brief essay I write both as a linguistic and a social anthropologist and as someone who enjoys and encourages collaborative publication. I intend some of my remarks for anthropologists in fields where collaborative writing is the marked case, that is, where it is relatively uncommon. My sense is that writing with others, while at times challenging, can afford some remarkable opportunities for contributing to the field. I'll outline some of the kinds of collaborative work current within cultural anthropology. Much of my commentary, however, addresses younger scholars more broadly across the field, as there are lots of problems—and possibilities—in common. I'll turn first to questions of authorship in the strict sense, then to a variety of genres of and outlets for collaborative work, to the question of recognition, and to the issue of audience, both immediate and in the more distant future. I'll close with some thoughts about new media and styles of scholarly communication and the possibilities and challenges they afford.

What could you write about collaboratively? With whom would you want to write? And, perhaps most importantly, why? Again, in some fields, research is assumed to be a necessarily collaborative activity, and shared authorship is taken to reflect these multiple contributions. In cultural and linguistic anthropology, however, it's a more open question. There may be many reasons for coauthorship: the examination of comparative cases, the consideration of a shared topic of interest from differing perspectives, the joint exploration of a set of related essays (as in shared introductions to an edited volume or special journal issue), or, perhaps, just the pleasure of working intensively with a colleague or colleagues. Coauthorship can be simultaneously exceptionally rewarding and a lot of hard, and at times fractious, work. Oral tradition in cultural anthropology suggests that those contemplating such writing should exchange MMPI profiles (or, in an earlier day, Rorschach results) before pursuing a shared project. This may be a slight exaggeration, but writing together requires a great deal of energy, patience, good humor, and the capacity to cut one another slack. Writing is rarely easy, even in the best of company, and, as scholars, we are necessarily deeply invested in what we produce and so can at times be more sensitive than necessary to delay and disagreement. At the same time, the rewards of joint work can be extraordinary.

In some subfields, authorship is shared among many people who are actively involved in the research being presented. This often includes one's supervisor (or the director of the relevant lab), colleagues working on complementary aspects of the research, and the occasional specialist in specific analytical techniques. Other collaborative articles might result from work shared among peers, and others can be the shared products of ethnographers or linguistic anthropologists and individual consultants from their field sites. In any case, before embarking on the project, negotiate what everyone's responsibilities will be. The clearer the prior agreement, the less likely any subsequent crankiness. Some divisions of work include the following: one person drafting and the other revising and developing the text further, alternating sections, or even jointly sitting at the keyboard. Working out your shared writing strategy beforehand, whatever it might be, is crucial. One further aspect to clarify beforehand in subfields where there isn't a prevailing norm is the question of who will be responsible for selecting publishing outlets for submission. In cultural anthropology, coauthored pieces often arise in the collective exuberance of oral presentations or shared commentary; the transition from performance to printed prose is at times very challenging.

In thinking about where you might want to submit a coauthored article, research and reflect. Where would you hope to have your article appear and why? Look at what sorts of articles, essays, or other genres particular journals appear to welcome and what different sections—for example, commentary, research reports, and the like—they might include. Looking for goodness of fit makes a difference. In a major journal in archaeology or biological anthropology, for example, collaborative authorship is more or less the norm, and a shared submission would be expected practice. In linguistic or cultural anthropology, however, you may need to think creatively about how most effectively to frame and structure a collaborative manuscript, and journals may vary in terms of how receptive they will be. As others in this volume note, taking submission guidelines and any "mission statements" seriously will aid you in getting a manuscript accepted. Editors and reviewers are asked to make difficult decisions among many promising submissions, and how a manuscript fits with the goals of the specific journal is always taken into serious account. What journals publish the kind of piece you and a colleague envision? And in what section? Beyond this, what are the characteristic styles and forms of such collaborative pieces? Pay close attention to "local" practice and protocols and try to find the publications that might most likely welcome a manuscript like yours. One size doesn't fit all, and journals vary widely.

There are lots of ways to structure a collaborative piece. The classic example would look like an ordinary article but acknowledge two or more scholarly authors rather than an individual. The nature of the collaboration can vary considerably. Many such articles draw upon each contributor's individual research, bringing the materials together for comparative purposes—or to triangulate toward a broader set of theoretical claims. Other pieces reflect fairly large-scale shared research drawing upon multiple actors and skills. The human genetics article coauthored by a lab group would be a classic instance of this method. Introductions to edited volumes or special issues are also often coauthored; good company and constructive interlocutors are particularly helpful in taking on such difficult projects. And some coauthored essays reflect a shared thinking through of complex issues and topics. One variation on this can draw upon one contributor's research but reflect a shared engagement in analyzing it (see, for a particularly generative example, Corsín Jiménez and Willerslev 2007). Other "rethinking" articles make explicit what Riles (2006: 1) has called the collaborative nature of "ethnographic conceptualization and response," that complex engagement both with our subjects and with each other as scholars that is characteristic of much anthropology. One particularly rich example of such engagement would be in collaborations between visual/multimedia anthropologists and more print-focused ones, or between those working from different perspectives within multimedia anthropology.

Occasionally individual scholars write collaboratively with their ethnographic consultants, a style of shared work I would like to see more frequently. One of my early articles was written jointly with a close collaborator from the community where I worked. Fascinated by a particular variety of scurrilous singing in the village, he had several notebooks of texts that he had transcribed as an adolescent. We jointly worked through the texts, located them ethnographically in both immediate context and the larger contours of community life, and negotiated the differences among local explanations, my colleague's own perspectives, and contemporary academic theory. It was both a truly joint production and an intellectually exhilarating experience, and it obviously depended in large part on such an engaged and capable colleague (Brenneis and Padarath 1975).

Other less ordinary collaborative publications are also possible. One strategy is juxtaposition, that is, bringing together several different sections—each obviously written by one author or another—in a single article. Such publications are not very common and require at least some framing to make it clear why they are in conversation with each other and in the same piece. Other collaborative articles take on an explicitly conversational form, some in the guise of interviews (which are rarely as straightforward as they might appear) and others as the apparent transcript of a dialogue. Several things are worth noting about experiments like these. First, they obviously require a journal or outlet whose editors are willing (or at times eager) to try dialogic pieces on for size. *Anthropology News* has proved remarkably hospitable to such forms, as, among more formal and full-length scholarly journals, has *Cultural Anthropology*. Other journals may well be less responsive. Second, the receptiveness of journals to such experiments often increases with the reputation and visibility of the collaborating authors. The social capital of established scholars may give them more license to try things out in print than might be afforded to younger anthropologists.

Another key kind of collaborative publishing is the coedited volume or special issue. Often arising from workshops, conferences, or meeting panels, such volumes draw directly upon the collective intellectual exuberance of intensive collegial conversation. They also at times prove to be particularly consequential in shaping the course of all the subfields of anthropology. Intellectually lively and influential as such larger collaborative projects may be, they also both require a great deal of work (including the amiable chivying of inevitably late contributors and the complex challenges of editing across a range of idiosyncratic styles) and all too often are not recognized institutionally as the significant scholarly accomplishments they indeed are. The preparation of—and finding an outlet for—such issues or volumes can be both time consuming (always requiring at least a year longer than expected) and frustrating. When considering a special issue, journals often require, quite appropriately, individual reviews of constituent manuscripts, and rarely do all the pieces get accepted. Taking on such coeditorial work makes much more sense for tenured academics than it does for younger scholars, not in terms of the imagination and acumen that would be brought to the project but because of the real and often disproportionate costs they involve.

I want to turn here to the issue of recognition, and especially of who is listed as an author—and how. For single-authored pieces, the byline is unproblematic. When multiple authors are involved, however, things can be complicated. When an article lists three or more authors, conventions vary by subdiscipline, or at times journal by journal, as to the order in which names should be listed. For instance, in biological research, the first-named author is the principal researcher. The second most prestigious location in the hard sciences is last (with the first author being the person who did the majority of the labor). Usually in these disciplines, footnotes explicitly signal the "corresponding author," wherever in the lineup this name might appear. Similarly the lab director or principal investigator for a major medical, practicing, or archaeological project (who might well not be the lead researcher for the specific article) may conventionally be listed in a specific place in the order. It's important to find out what a specific journal's customary practices are and follow them. If you are uncertain, you can consult with journal editors about their conventions. A footnote in which the roles played by different named authors are spelled out can acknowledge the specific ways in which each of the coauthors contributed to the research and writing. It's particularly helpful to designate who should receive page proofs (often the designation of "corresponding" author), if the journal will only send these to one scholar. Even if you don't annotate the byline, at least keep your own records clear on the division of labor (and funding) for possible future use. Such listings are not trivial; they also provide a particularly revelatory kind of data for looking at the underlying social organization of scientific research (see, for a particularly thought-provoking examination, Biagioli 2006).

A further aspect of recognition has to do with (and here I'll sound like the linguistic anthropologist I am) the conjunction you choose to use. Long series of authors' names often don't include a conjunction and are, rather, a list with commas. With fewer authors, however, a conjunction is customary, and it's worth remembering that "John Smith and Jane Brown" conveys a different sense of responsibility and credit than does "John Smith with Jane Brown." Occasional oral narratives circulate within the discipline about the consternation felt by those who claim to have been promised an *and* but ended up with a *with*. This can be a particularly significant issue in the case of pieces coauthored with community consultants.

One further aspect of coauthorship to keep in mind has to do with the characteristics of the audiences you expect for your piece. Some of these audiences are more or less expected and relatively immediate: scholars working in your subdiscipline, in your geographic region, or on related topics, or, in some cases, members of a broader public. Other audiences, however, often come into play in quite consequential ways. Among these are those institutional actors involved in hiring, evaluating, and making decisions about individual careers (and, at times, about the fates of the programs or departments in which they are based). The old adage that one must "publish or perish" has grown more pointed in recent years. Expectations as to the number of publications expected for tenure have risen dramatically, and the range of institutions sharing such increased expectations has expanded well beyond traditional research universities. At the same time, academic structures increasingly rely on numerical metrics for personnel decisions—not only the number of books and articles produced but also their ostensible value as (often quite inaccurately) measured by citation counts and other "impact factors." Such quantitative approaches have a stronger and more widely felt effect outside the United States, especially in the United Kingdom. In the United States, a continuing commitment in most institutions to expert and peer review—that is, to soliciting the opinions of outside scholars and making deliberative decisions about individual cases drawing upon such advice—balances the use of such metrics. I have logged many hours in such committee meetings, and the good news in regard to a collaborative publication is that it is rarely if ever treated as counting only half of what a single-authored article might. It generally—and appropriately—is treated as more or less commensurable with one's other publications. Some more specific points are worth making, however. First, evaluators might question coauthored work when it is not balanced by single-authored publications. Here, again, expectations differ considerably between more scientific and more humanistic styles of recognizing authorship. If your dossier has a lot of coauthored pieces, you might include notes for your tenure or review committee about your role and contributions. Second, it is important to be able to specify what one's contribution to any particular piece is. While this is often somewhat formulaic, that "both (or all) authors contributed equally" needs to be acknowledged, if not in the article itself, at least in any personnel document you might submit. Third, and this is more consequential in those subfields where multiple authorship is routine, tenure and promotion committees often look for evidence that the individuals under review have grown toward a scientific trajectory more or less autonomous from their graduate supervisor or lab director. Coauthorship with one's past advisor is taken as quite appropriate early on, but evidence of independent research topics and approaches is also increasingly expected—and a key measure is who one's coauthors are. In subdisciplines in which this trajectory is relevant, be mindful of the importance of moving from advisors to peers and advisees as coauthors.

Finally I want to note a paradox in regard to coauthorship. New media and new forms of scholarly communication, especially those afforded online, open a remarkable range of possibilities for creative and consequential collaborative scholarship. Despite my own technonaiveté, I've been very impressed by the liveliness and value of much of what's out there. At the same time, personnel committees, however innovative individuals may be as researchers, collectively act conservatively in reading the markers of scholarly accomplishment and ascertaining the value that they choose to recognize. The occasional opacity of the peer review process in online journals, for example, can limit their value in committee members' eyes, and the sorts of post-publication "peer response review" central to some online outlets tend not to be taken very seriously. Online publications are also at present difficult to translate into such metrics as citation counting and impact factors, or at least with the current quite limited apparatus generally used for such counts. Younger scholars tend to be both more savvy about and enthusiastic about online publication, and their participation in such venues will help move the rest of us, against the will of some but to the benefit of all of us, toward a better appreciation of—and perhaps more productive engagement with—such new media, and especially the opportunities for real-time collaboration they provide. But it's crucial that pretenure scholars find that Goldilocks point between currently "recognizable" scholarship and those emergent forms and genres that will shape our work in the future.

As a final thought, my message is to experiment, collaborate, and explore new forms of scholarly communication but also to remain mindful of the ways in which personnel evaluation tends to work.

FURTHER READING

Biagioli, Mario. "Documents of Documents: Scientists' Names and Scientific Claims." In *Documents: Artifacts of Modern Knowledge*, ed. Annelise Riles, 127–157. Ann Arbor: University of Michigan Press, 2006.

Brenneis, Donald, and Ram Padarath. "'About Those Scoundrels I'll Let Everyone Know': Challenge Singing in a Fiji Indian Community." *Journal of American Folklore* 88 (1975): 283–291.

Corsín Jiménez, Alberto, and Rane Willerslev. "'An Anthropological Concept of the Concept': Reversibility among the Siberian Yukaghirs." *Journal of the Royal Anthropological Institute* (N.S.) 13 (2006): 527–544.

Riles, Annelise. "Introduction: In Response." In *Documents: Artifacts of Modern Knowledge*, ed. Annelise Riles, 1–38. Ann Arbor: University of Michigan Press, 2006.

16

Online Opportunities and Challenges

Hugh W. Jarvis

In the context of the Internet—online publishing, digital communication, multimedia websites, and social media—all of your actions may impact your professional persona.

As a graduate student, you are naturally focused on finishing your degree, although probably keeping watch for ways to build your resume. So when you consider publishing, your first thoughts are likely about getting a conference paper accepted as a journal article or a chapter in an edited volume. Perhaps you are writing your dissertation and dream it will be released as a book. You may even be starting to consider life after graduate school and wondering how you can land a decent starting position, but I suspect you are not thinking about how all of your efforts now and in the future may impact you on the long road ahead.

This chapter is about your digital persona. Everything you do online has a direct influence on you as a person and on your reputation. Certainly your curriculum vitae and supporting documentation are the basis on which you are officially measured during recruitment and tenure review, but in truth, how you are perceived by your peers has an even broader impact, because it may affect your chance of being seriously considered for jobs, receiving funding, getting invited to sit on interesting panels or important committees, and other career-building opportunities.

I will briefly discuss your persona in this digital world and then explore opportunities to build your academic portfolio and strengthen your professional persona. Rather than cataloging dozens of online platforms, I use examples to demonstrate ways you can cultivate your persona while avoiding pitfalls that might damage your reputation.

YOUR PROFESSIONAL PERSONA

As you build your academic portfolio, remember you are simultaneously constructing your professional persona, so make your choices wisely. Be sure your ambitions are less about beating your peers to scarce positions than about being acknowledged as the best candidate in the first place.

Billions of readers could read your words online. This is a wonderful thing but perilous too. Your conduct may be seen outside of the context you originally intended, or even be broken into distorted fragments that are widely disseminated in ways you never anticipated. Everything you type is readily accessible to the world, possibly forever, even in situations you thought were private. Take it for granted that your words and pictures will be intentionally and accidentally shared with all of your friends and colleagues and may also be visible in ways that can unexpectedly enhance or corrode your character in the eyes of people who may never meet you in person. Assume your online actions will be seen by everyone and act accordingly. Not only is damage hard to undo, you likely will never know where to make amends anyway. So do everything possible to ensure your impact is positive.

My reasoning should be obvious. As a budding scholar, your worth is primarily based on opinions held by those with whom you interact. The old cliché that you can always relocate and start over with a clean slate no longer applies. On the Internet, an ever-growing record of your past actions follows you everywhere. This conduct may be quickly exposed during intentional or even accidental searches, or in new services that actively catalog people's online life histories for those who know where to look. Until it becomes second nature, make a conscious effort to appreciate how your words will be received and how bystanders might view your behavior in general. Before you act, think through what you are trying to communicate and how you can best achieve that goal. One quick trick is to emulate the behavior of someone you respect. If you have any second thoughts or if your words might be controversial or misinterpreted, get a second opinion, revise your message at least three times, and then sleep on it. There is seldom need for an instant reply, and while you consider your own response, someone else may chime in with better information, saving you the effort or even revealing unforeseen pitfalls you would have encountered. Beyond the occasional emoticon, such as the smiley face, computer interaction lacks nonverbal cues that convey nuance and actually communicate the vast majority of your message during a face-to-face conversation. So choose your words carefully, explain your reasoning, and make your messages easy to read. Never make harsh remarks; not only are they destructive and a waste of your time, but they are also unlikely to have useful impact; and, most importantly, they may cause your reputation permanent harm.

Further, consider the ultimate goal of your engagement in each forum where you have a presence. Are you hoping to extend your network? Would you like to establish yourself as an authority on certain topics? Are you seeking advice on your research? These objectives should guide your interactions for that forum since the behavior you express now may impact how you are treated in return, now and in the future.

The goal is to calculate wisely, not to be conservative; to be focused and smart, not manipulative. This clarity will help you to stay focused and economize your limited time. It will also maximize the positive impact on your persona. Try to be associated with admirable qualities like credibility, authority, reason, collegiality, and good humor. Be the consummate professional. These associations will steadily grow around your identity, lend credibility to your actions, and ultimately provide opportunities that might otherwise be offered to someone else. Karma is real.

These tips are also applicable in daily interactions off-line and in your writing itself, and although a great deal more can be written on this topic, hopefully I have opened the door. Now let's turn to your portfolio.

YOUR PROFESSIONAL PORTFOLIO

Ideally by now you have found a supportive mentor who can help you to choose a research focus that not only fits your interests but will also merit funding and future employment. If so, some of the comments here may repeat the advice from your mentor.

The summary of your accomplishments will be your curriculum vitae, and you should always make a current copy available online. In addition, keep a current dossier with details of your academic and professional career and your scholarly credentials (conference details, awards, publications, and other qualifications) and save evaluations, letters of praise, citation or usage statistics, and any other indication of your impact because our current business-oriented society demands these assessments. Doing this as you go will save you time digging these details up later after they get buried or replacing those that are lost completely, and may help remind you where your priorities lie in terms of advancing yourself as a professional.

If you are interested in an academic job, your efforts must be aligned with hiring and tenure requirements. You may find the chapters in part II helpful in evaluating what "counts" in terms of publishing within various disciplines. Discover the specific criteria that actually count toward employment and advancement. Appreciate that these requirements vary greatly between departments and also will change over time as social norms evolve and new administrators come into power. The bottom line is that each department uses its own metrics to weigh a prospect's merit. Sometimes each committee member may even have a different set of criteria (certainly they will apply their own interpretation), while in other universities they rely on ranked lists of journals and publishers and required numbers of publications in each. In some schools, this information seems to be sacred knowledge; in others, it is not formalized or even consistently applied. Start by discovering what your own department uses—ask your chair and your colleagues about their expectations.

Where it comes to your publishing record, I suspect their standards will seem extremely conservative (see Harley et al. 2010). Most likely they will value publications from large commercial and university presses or articles in key journals, those that have peer review, large circulation, high citation rates, and are well respected. With the exception of visual anthropologists, assume most committee members will have difficulty seeing merit in smaller or nontraditional journals, self-publications, or new formats like websites, blogs, or even multimedia. Further, since impact assessments are based on citation data, and many "nontraditional" publications are not (yet) tracked by citation software, you may have great difficulty establishing their worth. If you plan to get credit for work on online projects or in other new media, expect an uphill battle. Since new media impact may be indirect and fleeting, document your work while you can and build in tools to track its use (e.g., feedback forms and Google Analytics codes). Also keep copies of praise (e.g., was your work mentioned in a textbook, was it the foundation for another grant, or did your efforts assist a colleague?).

Beyond your scholarly output, your persona has significant impact here. Given the choice, departments naturally lean toward hiring people with good personal and professional credentials, as well as a suitable resume. The positive opinions of your peers and their colleagues may bring you to the attention of academic departments in the first place, as well as help move you onto their short list. While your position as an expert in your focus area will certainly require traditional scholarly publishing activities, it can be honed by networking and scholarly interaction with your colleagues, which is easily conducted through online activities.

But once again, successful academics stay focused on hiring and tenure requirements. While tenured professors have earned great freedom, the rest of us need to be very conscious of the steps to earning that status, especially when budgets are shrinking and job seekers are so numerous. Young scholars tend to be dreamers, pioneering open access, new media, and collaborative ventures—the Web is full of opportunities to explore these paths. You may get some credit for these as service efforts, but they are unlikely to get you hired or tenured in most departments; even worse, they suck up an enormous amount of your energy. The road to tenure is brutally short, but happily, once you have gained job security, you can work to change the system from the inside.

CHANGE IS COMING (SLOWLY)

I have set a gloomy picture, advocating against much of the fun and creative spark of the online world. However, academia is slowly embracing new forms of scholarship. More journals are going online, for example, and some are abandoning their paper editions. While the online migration has a large impact on the economics of publishing, it has an even greater impact on accessibility. You already know how much information is at your fingertips just in Google. Find ways to make your scholarship more visible to your peers. The products of all your hard work should be widely and easily accessible, not locked inside expensive or exclusive publications. For instance, your publications should be readily available in all major search engines and scholarly databases, discoverable through subject keywords and full-text indexing, not just your name and title words, and you may wish to evaluate your scholarly participation based on this kind of visibility. Simply put, will your published work show up in a Google search by its title, or, ideally, through searches for significant words that occur in your abstract, or—best of all—the full text of your publication? If your colleagues do literature searches in common scholarly databases, will your work be listed in the results? Use your subject librarians here. They know the answers to these questions, because they use them to make purchasing decisions. In publications that have successfully created highly visible online inventories, colleagues and the public are able to discover publications during routine searches and to view title and abstract details, which is enough to know whether they would benefit from reading the entire article, even if the full text were only available for a fee or by subscription. This relatively simple publishing practice greatly enhances the potential impact of your work, while also serving the publisher's needs, and is a reasonable return for your extensive labor as an author.

As you write, consider how accessible your work is to the largest potential audience. There is no need to "dumb down" your writing, but overly complicated or excessive jargon actually interferes with the transfer of knowledge. Try to write in the simplest and clearest manner possible. Your audience will not be impressed by your eloquence if they fail to download your article because it appears to be irrelevant for their needs. Instead of sophisticated phrasings, adopt the language that your preferred audience expects, especially for your title, abstract, and introductory paragraphs. Remember that most of your colleagues will encounter your publications not while scanning a shelf or by browsing a table of contents but during searches, and a clear title and abstract will be the hooks that encourage them to read further. Ideally, repeat the most important keywords in your title, abstract, and introduction to boost their occurrence in search engine indexes. This simple trick of keyword loading (part of "search engine optimization") will help ensure that your work floats to the top of relevant searches.

Further, if each of us clearly labeled the copyright status of all our work, including unpublished materials, scholars would have no difficulty establishing the legal limits to their use. This would provide more legal protection and save money for copyright clearance, a must for classroom use, while opening up your work for acceptable use and reuse by your colleagues around the world. The international legal standards developed by the Creative Commons (see "Resources") provide a flexible solution for most situations—I strongly encourage you to apply them in all of your work. Chapter 13 on author agreements covers these concepts in more detail.

What about Open Access?

Over the past few years, there has been passionate debate about "open-access" publishing. It is often thought to mean that you should be able to publish and read your colleagues' publications without any cost, and perhaps to use your own work in any way you want, despite others (e.g., your editor and publisher) investing their own resources into its publication. Advocates promote the value of wide-open information sharing and decry the evils of an industry that devours limited budgets, exploits the unpaid labor of scholars, and prices publications out of general reach, just to generate stockholder dividends. Moderates caution that publishing must be funded somehow, and large-scale "free" models are fiscally impractical and unsustainable.

There has been some success at more open models. For example, in the physical and medical sciences, grant money (i.e., tax dollars) typically underwrites publishing costs, allowing articles to be released for free. This is generally not possible in the social sciences, where grants are fewer and smaller. If you are fortunate enough to win a grant from the National Institutes of Health or the National Science Foundation, include author payment fees in your budget. Using these grant funds, authors can pay production costs up front (called the "gold open access"); articles can then become free to all. Smaller journals have achieved some success, absorbing costs into departmental budgets and using unpaid staff, but these are risky ventures and may collapse in lean years. External funds are rarely available to pay for routine operating costs. Scholarly societies, such as the American Anthropological Association (AAA), are beginning to explore alternative funding models and ways to release more of their content for free or at reduced rates.

There is a work-around: "green open access" is a practical solution we should all promote. When you submit a manuscript for publication, request an author agreement that allows you to retain a personal copy of the postprint (i.e., the peer-reviewed final draft) on a local institutional repository. You may make this copy available at your discretion, supporting open access and commercial publishing in the process. The AAA supports this practice for all of its journals, and the association is thus rated as a "green publisher" by Project RoMEO (see "Resources," including the Budapest Open Access Initiative's "Self-Archiving FAQ").

No, this is not the pretty, published version, but the entire content is now freely available for anyone to use, and this is usually what scholars actually want. The publishing world is slowly evolving, and we can anticipate changes, including broader access to information. In the meantime, protect your best chances to get hired and gain tenure by publishing in the highest-ranked, most visible journals you can that Project RoMEO rates as "green." Publishing within highly ranked journals may protect you at this sensitive stage of your career, and finding those that allow you to deposit postprints in repositories will help expand your reputation and persona. (If your interest lies in publishing in purely open-access journals, the Directory of Open Access Journals provides the most comprehensive list available—see "Resources.")

If you are not aiming for an academic job, your overall persona—your scholarly and nonscholarly publishing record and your professional track record in general—may be very important in making you desirable for a position in a nongovernmental organization, museum, or cultural resources management agency. All of the advice here is equally applicable to careers outside of academia, with the proviso that the emphasis switches to your ability to produce results of value to a prospective employer, not just a weighty list of scholarly publications. You will need to show that you can balance your writing with fieldwork (emphasis on the *work*) and show your ability to research topics that are of value to the public and government interests rather than attacking more esoteric topics of deeper interest to your academic peers. Also, by entering the business world, you should follow an even stricter code of conduct than in academia, at least until you do get hired. Johansson (2011) provides some useful tips for appropriate conduct on Twitter, although the concepts can be applied to social media in general.

USING THE WEB EFFECTIVELY

So how do you do more of the stuff online that will help you and your career, whether that be in the academy or outside of it? You can use the Internet to build networks, connections that will assist during all stages of your research, then later to develop your ideas into grants and publications. The Web is also a priceless source of career and research advice and an excellent platform for collaboration with your peers. For additional tips, see Posner et al. (2011).

The Web as a Tool for Connecting

The Web provides endless opportunities for participating with other people in discussions and information sharing. Spend your energies where they will do you the most good, and allocate your online time wisely. This may sound cold, but it is sensible to allocate your precious time among those you most wish to learn from, collaborate with, and impress. Assuming your efforts are productive, this will also do your colleagues the most good. In the process, it will elevate your visibility and strengthen your credentials so that they will have the most impact. Look for venues frequented by those who share your research interests.

Take the time to establish a professional profile with current contact information in each website you frequent. They are really an ecosystem, so consider the impact of what you reveal in that setting, as well as overall. Consistently reinforce who you are by attaching a name and face to your words (use a real picture!), and ensure that people can learn more about you, to better understand your actions, perhaps to ask you a question, or to explore research opportunities of their own. Remember that others are looking for potential collaborators; they may well be seeking someone just like you. Keep your profile current by updating your publications, activities, and awards regularly.

Look for opportunities to strengthen your professional networks. A strong foundation of collaborators who appreciate your scholarly interests may facilitate your ability to do research and publish your work, plus this interaction may strengthen your persona where it has the greatest impact. The Web helps you keep track of colleagues and stay visible yourself and provides online tools and communities that facilitate interaction.

In Web terms, social networking just means large groups of people interacting, sometimes *really* large groups, and there are many online platforms that support these activities. In the interest of brevity, I will contrast Facebook with LinkedIn.

Facebook.com reports over 400 million users worldwide; but adoption varies tremendously, and most older, more accomplished scholars barely know it exists. This gap is shrinking, but it will be years before the people who run departments and control search and tenure committees fully embrace its use.

While LinkedIn.com has "only" 65 million members worldwide, it is rapidly becoming de rigueur for corporate connectivity, including public institutions and private firms where many of our colleagues work or seek jobs. While Facebook encourages casual chatter, LinkedIn is quite formal. Where Facebook attempts to befriend the entire world, LinkedIn connects with fellow employees, people you actually knew, and those in related professions, to assist in advancement and relocation to better positions.

I suggest you maintain a LinkedIn profile as a routine procedure to show you are a serious professional and to extend your professional visibility. Unlike Facebook, it obeys European Union privacy standards and is clearly intended to build trust, not advertising revenue, and new features allow you to attach blog postings, documents, presentations, and reading lists to your profile, generating more return for your efforts elsewhere. The site is also experimenting with collaborative workspaces.

Both platforms alert you to changes in status (location, employment) of your peers, so you can stay in touch. However, Facebook may be a professional liability. Facebook makes your personal activities broadly visible (a potential audience of millions!), blurring boundaries between personal, professional, and public life. Keep your personal life limited to close friends and family. This may reduce unwanted attention and keep potentially embarrassing behavior off your own site. Since you cannot control what others post, you may be wise to keep their activities at a distance. For more Facebook advice, see Perlmutter (2009a, 2009b) and Hara (2011).

Exercise great caution when you use any social networking site. Not only do employers browse a prospect's profiles, but even supposedly private messages leak out. Academics have been sanctioned for their online comments. Consider what you post very carefully. An innocuous description of a hobby or event may cause alarm when accidentally encountered by your chair or colleagues, your students, or their parents.

The Web as a Source of Information

Unlike social networking sites that encourage mass membership, some websites focus on topics of interest to anthropologists and offer tremendous opportunities for networking and collaboration. Why build your own network the hard way when these online communities are already populated by people with common interests? These sites may be ideal places to engage in focused discussion of real interest to you, as well as to broaden your network. Excellent examples in the spring of 2011 include the Open Anthropology Cooperative (open exchange on current topics); Paleoanthro (primatology, paleoanthropology, and archaeology); the SfAA Community Network (for applied and practicing anthropologists); and ArchaeoSeek (the "social network for archaeologists"). See "Resources" for links.

Also consider e-mail discussion groups or "listservs." Some of these are extremely active and popular among older scholars and those with limited connectivity in rural areas and overseas. There are several dozen for anthropology and as many for other disciplines that may be relevant to you. Listservs offer threaded discussions (continuous, linked discussions on one specific topic), centralized maintenance of addresses (no need to search out or update contacts), and searchable archives of older discussions (knowledge gained from past conversations is retained)—all invaluable features that social networking platforms cannot provide. Anthro-L (general anthropology) and Arch-L (general archaeology) are long-standing examples that predate the Web (see "Resources").

While I discourage active blogging by young scholars—it requires a major investment of your precious time—several established blogs may be worth monitoring for the information that is posted, but perhaps even more for the secondary discussions that emerge. The mission of *Savage Minds* is to make anthropology more visible to the public and provide a forum for current topics in our discipline. Those with an interest in the military or academic freedom and ethics may enjoy *Zero Anthropology*, while *Open Access Anthropology* advocates discussion of alternative publishing models. *Neuroanthropology* covers the intersection of anthropology with neuroscience. The AAA has its own forum, hosting discussion of topics of particular interest to its members. Finally, the *Chronicle of Higher Education*'s *ProfHacker* is an outstanding source of "tips, tutorials, and commentary on pedagogy, productivity, and technology in higher education" written by faculty and students. Monitor their latest postings via the free *Chronicle* e-mail alert; then mine their archives for useful teaching and research tools. A new project called *GradHacker* was just launched and may provide similar information. (See "Resources.")

The bottom line is that Internet forums may have large numbers of users from around the world, each with a common interest, and these participants are well accustomed to new colleagues entering the conversations. Therefore, these are ideal places to get your feet wet in scholarly discourse, to gain knowledge, and to start networks. These are public spaces where you can easily learn a great deal by monitoring ongoing discussions ("lurking") or actively exploring research ideas and soliciting information from your peers. Such forums may present opportunities to develop your online persona and to do service by sharing your knowledge with the public at large, but be careful about your time investment.

The Web as a Platform for Collaboration

A wide variety of web-based tools may make collaboration easier. Telefony software such as Skype.com provides free voice and video conferencing, and new features like a whiteboard tool offer economical ways to conference with your peers on research. Multimedia-sharing sites like Flickr.com and the infamous YouTube.com provide ways to quickly share images and videos, and also to easily embed them in other web platforms, and they provide more secure storage than your vulnerable computer. You can also easily limit access to sensitive information.

Keep an eye on the ever-growing Google.com suite, including Google Docs, which provides a powerful platform for the creation of documents, spreadsheets, slideshow presentations, and now also drawings. These objects can be converted from locally created files or can be created online, by you alone or in collaboration, and the end product can then easily and securely be shared with an audience you specify. The software is so robust that authors can edit the same document simultaneously. The opportunities for asynchronous or even synchronous collaboration are already enormous, and while these tools currently provide only a "lite" version of their MS Office cousins, Google is rapidly adding new features. And it is all free.

CONCLUSION

The Internet offers many opportunities but as many liabilities. Chart your interactions thoughtfully, considering their effect on your professional persona. Look out for chances to build relationships with colleagues who share common interests, or connections that support your personal needs. Explore the many web tools that will make your work and collaboration with your peers so much easier. And when you publish, choose the "greenest" journals possible.

FURTHER READING

Hara, Billie. "Think before You Tweet (or Blog or Update a Status)." *Chronicle of Higher Education*, February 23, 2011. http://chronicle.com/blogs/profhacker/think-before-you-tweet-or-blog-or-update-a-status/30949.

Harley, Diane, Sophia Krzys Acord, Sarah Earl-Novell, Shannon Lawrence, and C. Judson King. *Assessing the Future Landscape of Scholarly Communication: An Exploration of Faculty Values and Needs in Seven Disciplines*. Berkeley: University of California Center for Studies in Higher Education, 2010. http://cshe.berkeley.edu/publications/publications.php?id=351.

Johansson, Mike. "Why Are You on Twitter? A 'Twitter 101' Lesson." *SocialMedia Today*, May 30, 2011. http://socialmediatoday.com/mike-johansson/300892/twitter-101-why-are-you-twitter.

Perlmutter, David D. "Facebooking Your Way out of Tenure." *Chronicle of Higher Education*, July 3, 2009a. http://chronicle.com/article/Facebooking-Your-Way-Out-of/46951.

Perlmutter, David D. "Facebooking for the Tenure Track." *Chronicle of Higher Education*, September 4, 2009b. http://chronicle.com/article/Facebooking-for-the-Tenure/48218.

Posner, Miriam, Stewart Varner, and Brian Croxall. "Creating Your Web Presence: A Primer for Academics." *Chronicle of Higher Education*, February 14, 2011.

http://chronicle.com/blogs/profhacker/creating-your-web-presence-a-primer-for-academics/30458.

RESOURCES

AAA web forum
http:// blog.aaanet.org
Anthropology Resources on the Internet (including Listservs)
http://aaanet.org/resources
ArchaeoSeek
http://archaeoseek.ning.com
Budapest Open Access Initiative's "Self-Archiving FAQ"
http://www.eprints.org/openaccess/self-faq
http://chronicle.com/blog/ProfHacker/27
Creative Commons
http://creativecommons.org
Directory of Open Access Journals (open-access anthropology journals)
http://www.doaj.org/doaj?cpid=124&func=subject
Google Analytics (free website usage tracking)
http://google.com/analytics
Google Docs (free productivity tools)
http://docs.google.com
GradHacker blog (academic and professional advice)
http://www.gradhacker.org
Neuroanthropology blog
http://blogs.plos.org/neuroanthropology/
Open Access Anthropology blog
http://blog.openaccessanthropology.org
Open Anthropology Cooperative
http://openanthcoop.ning.com
Paleoanthro
http://groups.yahoo.com/community/paleoanthro
ProfHacker blog (academic and professional advice)
Project RoMEO (rates "green" publishers)
http://www.sherpa.ac.uk/romeo
Savage Minds blog
http://SavageMinds.org
Society for Applied Anthropology Community
http://community.sfaa.net
Zero Anthropology blog
http://ZeroAnthropology.net

Appendix A: Peer-Reviewed Journals

The following is a list of peer-reviewed journals and their ISSNs that published content in English in the spring of 2011. Researchers should read recent issues of specific journals to understand their mission, scope, and style. Some of the journals focus on a specific theoretical framework or publish content in only specific subdisciplines or geographical areas. The length, format, and type of articles vary widely as well.

In addition to looking at content, prospective authors should look at the rankings for the journals they consider, the average time submissions are under consideration, the time to publish, and the journals' reputations. The chapters in part II on select subdisciplines provide more information as well.

Africa: The Journal of the International African Institute	0001-9720
American Anthropologist	0002-7294
American Antiquity	0002-7316
American Ethnologist	0094-0496
American Indian Culture and Research Journal	0161-6463
American Journal of Archaeology	0002-9114
American Journal of Human Biology	1042-0533
American Journal of Physical Anthropology	0002-9483
American Journal of Primatology	0275-2565
Annals of Human Biology	0301-4460
Annals of Practicing Anthropology (formerly titled *NAPA Bulletin*)	2153-957X (1556-4797)
Annual Review of Anthropology	0084-6570
Anthropoetics: The Electronic Journal of Generative Anthropology	1083-7264
Anthropologica	0003-5459
Anthropological Forum: A Journal of Social Anthropology and Comparative Sociology	0066-4677

Anthropological Linguistics	0003-5483
Anthropological Quarterly	0003-5491
Anthropological Science	0918-7960
Anthropological Theory	1463-4996
Anthropologischer Anzeiger	0003-5548
Anthropology and Archeology of Eurasia	1061-1959
Anthropology & Education Quarterly	0161-7761
Anthropology and Humanism	0193-5615
Anthropology & Medicine	1364-8470
Anthropology in Action	0967-201X
Anthropology of Consciousness	1053-4202
Anthropology of Work Review	0883-024X
Anthropos	0257-9774
Anthrozoos: A Multidisciplinary Journal of the Interactions of People and Animals	0892-7936
Antiquity	0003-598X
Applied Linguistics	1477-450X
Archaeologies: Journal of the World Archaeological Congress	1555-8622
Archeological Papers of the American Anthropology Association	1551-823X
Arctic Anthropology	0066-6939
Asian Perspectives: The Journal of Archaeology for Asia and the Pacific	0066-8435
Bijdragen Tot De Taal-Land-En Volkenkunde/Journal of the Humanities and Social Sciences of Southeast Asia and Oceania	0006-2294
Body and Society	1460-3632
Childhood	1461-7013
Chungara: Revista de Antropologia Chilena	0716-1182
City & Society	0893-0465
Collegium Anthropologicum	0350-6134
Comparative Studies in Society and History	0010-4175
Critique of Anthropology	0308-275X
Cross-Cultural Research: The Journal of Comparative Social Sciences	1069-3971
Cultural Anthropology	0886-7356
Cultural Dynamics	1461-7048
Cultural Studies	0950-2386
Culture, Agriculture, Food & Environment (formerly *Culture & Agriculture*)	2153-9553 (1048-4876)
Culture, Medicine and Psychiatry	0165-005X
Current Anthropology	0011-3204
Dialectical Anthropology	0304-4092
Ethnicities	1741-2706
Ethnography	1466-1381
Ethnohistory	0014-1801
Ethnomusicology	0014-1836

Ethnos	0014-1844
Ethos: Journal of the Society for Psychological Anthropology	0091-2131
European Journal of Archaeology	1461-9571
Evolutionary Anthropology	1060-1538
Field Methods	1525-822X
Food and Foodways: Explorations in the History and Culture of Human Nourishment	0740-9710
Food Culture and Society: An International Journal of Multidisciplinary Research	1552-8014
Global Networks: A Journal of Transnational Affairs	1471-0374
Homo: Journal of Comparative Human Biology	0018-442X
Human Ecology: An Interdisciplinary Journal	0018-442X
Human Nature: An Interdisciplinary Biosocial Perspective	1045-6767
Human Organization	0018-7259
Inter-Asia Cultural Studies	1469-8447
International Journal of American Linguistics	0020-7071
International Journal of Cultural Studies	1460-356X
International Journal of Historical Archaeology	1092-7697
International Journal of Osteoarchaeology	1047-482X
International Journal of Primatology	0164-0291
Journal of American Folklore	0021-8715
Journal of Anthropological Archaeology	0278-4165
Journal of Anthropological Research	0091-7710
Journal of Archaeological Method and Theory	1072-5369
Journal of Archaeological Research	1059-0161
Journal of Archaeological Science	0305-4403
Journal of Asian and African Studies	0021-9096
Journal of Consumer Culture	1469-5405
Journal of Family History: Studies in Family, Kinship, Gender, and Demography	0363-1990
Journal of Field Archaeology	0093-4690
Journal of Human Evolution	0047-2484
Journal of Latin American and Caribbean Anthropology	1935-4932
Journal of Linguistic Anthropology	1055-1360
Journal of Mammalian Evolution	1064-7554
Journal of Material Culture	1359-1835
Journal of Peasant Studies: Critical Perspectives on Rural Politics and Development	1743-9361
Journal of Political Ecology: Case Studies in History and Society	1073-0451
Journal of the Royal Anthropological Institute	1359-0987
Journal of Social Archaeology	1469-6053
Journal of Sociolinguistics	1360-6441
Journal of Visual Culture	1470-4129
Journal of World-Systems Research	1076-156X
Language	0097-8507

Language in Society	0047-4045
Latin American Antiquity	1045-6635
Linguistic Inquiry	0024-3892
Mana: Studies in Social Anthropology	0104-9313
Mankind Quarterly	0025-2344
Medical Anthropology Quarterly: International Journal for the Analysis of Health	0745-5194
Museum Anthropology	0892-8339
Museum Anthropology Review	1938-5145
Oceania	0029-8077
PoLAR: Political and Legal Anthropology Review	1081-6976
Primates	0032-8332
Public Culture	0899-2363
Qualitative Research	1468-7941
Race & Class: A Journal on Racism, Empire and Globalisation	0306-3968
Science	0193-4511
Science as Culture	0950-5431
Social Anthropology/Anthropologie Sociale	0964-0282
Social Networks	0378-8733
Space and Culture	1206-3312
Theory, Culture & Society	0263-2764
Time & Society	0961-463X
Transforming Anthropology	1051-0559
Visual Anthropology	0894-9468
Visual Anthropology Review	1058-7187
Visual Communication	1470-3572
Visual Studies	1472-586X
World Archaeology	0043-8243
Written Communication	0741-0883
Zeitschrift Fur Ethnologie [Journal of Anthropology]	0044-2666

Appendix B: Publishers That Publish Anthropology Monographs

The listed publishing houses historically publish monographs by anthropologists. The list is accurate as of spring 2011; however, publishers may change focus. The list was compiled using several sources including the American Association of University Presses, the Society for Scholarly Publishing, the Association of Learned and Professional Society Publishers, the American Association of Publishers' Professional/Scholarly Publishing Division, and those presses that have participated in the book exhibits at the recent annual meetings of the American Anthropological Association and the Society for American Archaeology.

Although the discipline of Anthropology is broad in scope, it is important to note that many publishers specialize in a narrowly focused area. Explore the publisher's website and current book lists to see whether they publish material similar to what you hope to publish.

Alexander Street Press
AltaMira Press
American University in Cairo Press, the
Amsterdam University Press
Athabasca University Press
Beacon Press
Berg Publishers
Berghahn Books
Brookings Institution Press, the
Cambridge University Press
Chatham House
Chinese University Press, the
Columbia University Press
Cornell University Press
Duke University Press
Dumbarton Oaks Publications
Edinburgh University Press
Edwin Mellen Press, the
Elsevier Books
Equinox Publishing
Fordham University Press
Georgetown University Press
Guilford Press
Haiduk Press
Harvard University Press
Indiana University Press

Lawrence & Wishart
Left Coast Press
Leuven University Press
Liverpool University Press
Lynne Rienner Publishers
M. E. Sharpe
Manchester University Press
Maney Publishing
McGill-Queen's University Press
Michigan State University Press
Minnesota Historical Society Press
Modern Language Association book publications program
New York University Press
Nicholas Brealey Publishing
Northern Illinois University Press
Ohio University Press
Oklahoma University Press
Oxford University Press
Palgrave Macmillan
Pearson (including Allyn & Bacon and Prentice Hall)
Penguin Group (USA)
Penn State University Press, the
Perseus Books Group
Princeton University Press
Rand Corporation
Routledge/Taylor & Francis Group
Rutgers University Press
Sage Publications
Society for American Archaeology Press
Springer
Stanford University Press
State University of New York Press
Stylus Publishing
Sydney University Press
Temple University Press
Texas A&M University Press
Transaction Publishers
University of Alabama Press
University of Alaska Press
University of Arizona Press
University of British Columbia Press
University of Calgary Press
University of California Press
University of Chicago Press
University of Hawai'i Press
University of Illinois Press, the
University of Iowa
University of Malaya Press
University of Minnesota Press
University of Nebraska Press
University of Nevada Press
University of New Mexico Press
University of North Carolina Press, the
University of Pennsylvania Press
University of Puerto Rico Press
University of Tennessee Press, the
University of Texas Press
University of Tokyo Press
University of Toronto Press
University of Utah Press
University of Washington Press
University of Wisconsin Press
University Press of Colorado
University Press of Florida
Vanderbilt University Press
W. W. Norton & Company
Wadsworth Cengage Learning
Walter de Gruyter
Waveland Press
Wayne State University Press
Wesleyan University Press
Wiley-Blackwell
Wilfrid Laurier University Press
Woodrow Wilson International Center for Scholars
Wormwood Press
Yale University Press

About the Editors and Contributors

Catherine Besteman is professor and chair of anthropology at Colby College. She is author/editor of six books and organized the Somali Bantu Experience website.

Peter Biella is professor of anthropology and director of the Visual Anthropology emphasis at San Francisco State University. He is a past president of the Society for Visual Anthropology and occasional editor of *Visual Anthropology Review*.

Tom Boellstorff is professor of anthropology at the University of California, Irvine, and the editor in chief of *American Anthropologist*.

Don Brenneis is professor of anthropology at University of California, Santa Cruz. Brenneis coedits the *Annual Review of Anthropology*.

Mary Bucholtz is professor of linguistics at University of California, Santa Barbara. She is a former editor of the *Journal of Linguistic Anthropology*.

Sarah Caro is a publisher in the Social Sciences Division at Wiley-Blackwell in Oxford, United Kingdom. She is the author of *How to Publish Your PhD*.

Paul N. Edwards is a professor in the School of Information and the Department of History at the University of Michigan. He directs the Science, Technology and Society Program.

Linda Forman has worked as an archaeologist in the Midwest and Mexico. She is currently senior copy editor of *American Ethnologist*; previously she held similar positions with *Medical Anthropology Quarterly* and *Midcontinental Journal of Archaeology*.

Paul A. Garber is professor of anthropology, LAS global studies, and Latin American and Caribbean studies at the University of Illinois at Urbana-Champaign. He is also executive editor of the *American Journal of Primatology*.

Peter Givler is executive director of the Association of American University Presses. Givler is also president of the International Federation of Scholarly Publishers and an executive board member of the International Publishers Association where he also chairs the Copyright Committee.

William Green is director of the Logan Museum of Anthropology and adjunct professor of anthropology at Beloit College. He was the founding president of the Midwest Archaeological Conference Inc. and served as editor of its journal, the *Midcontinental Journal of Archaeology.*

Ricky S. Huard is in charge of intellectual property at the Gladys W. and David H. Patton College of Education and Human Services at Ohio University.

Hugh W. Jarvis is cybrarian for the University at Buffalo's Office of University Communications, which oversees marketing communications as well as print and digital publications. With a scholarly background in anthropological archaeology, Jarvis has created and run a wide range of online services, including Internet journals, directories, and way-finding tools, and is a member of the American Anthropological Association's Committee on the Future of Print and Electronic Publishing.

Jason E. Miller is a doctoral candidate in applied anthropology at the University of South Florida who specializes in visual and participatory approaches to anthropology. Miller holds the student seat on the executive board of the American Anthropological Association and is a former president of the National Association of Student Anthropologists.

Oona Schmid is director of publishing at the American Anthropological Association, the publisher of 20-plus journals and AnthroSource.

John K. Trainor is a doctoral candidate in applied anthropology at the University of South Florida who specializes in biocultural anthropology and preventing childhood obesity. He is a former president of the National Association of Student Anthropologists.

Cecilia Vindrola Padros is a doctoral candidate in applied anthropology at the University of South Florida. Her dissertation focuses on the experiences of pediatric oncology patients and their parents while accessing health services within the public health system in Argentina.

Tim Wallace is an associate professor in the Department of Sociology and Anthropology at North Carolina State University. Wallace is president of the National Association for the Practice of Anthropology and former editor of the *NAPA Bulletin* and is also editor of the Society for Applied Anthropology newsletter.

Linda M. Whiteford is professor of anthropology and vice provost for Program Development and Review at the University of South Florida. She is a former president of the Society for Applied Anthropology.

CPSIA information can be obtained at www.ICGtesting.com
Printed in the USA
BVOW010843011111

274955BV00006B/2/P

9 780759 121089